The Treacherous Snows

The author at the Horombo Huts. Mt. Kilimanjaro in the distance

The Treacherous Snows

Andrew C. Hartzell

VANTAGE PRESS
New York

Published by Vantage Press, Inc.
516 West 34th Street, New York, New York 10001

Manufactured in the United States of America
ISBN: 0-533-10527-7

Library of Congress Catalog Card No.: 92-94301

0 9 8 7 6 5 4 3 2 1

For Mary Lee, with love

Contents

Foreword

Not since the Swiss Family Robinson's holiday took an unexpected course have family vacations been a subject of general interest. Most are placid and restorative, the events routine regardless of locale. That, indeed, is their charm and purpose, for *vacatio*—to be empty of duty or obligation—is the opposite of testing and challenge.

Our vacations have followed such a pattern, spiced with occasional excitement. One afternoon we were hiking on an open slope in Glacier National Park. A meteorite came up the valley, passed overhead, seeming near enough to touch, and disappeared beyond the mountain with a puff of smoke and an eerie boom. We later learned it was the only celestial visitor in this century to have entered the earth's atmosphere and skipped out again into space. The size of a football field, it had created a sensation across several western states; we happened to be in a natural amphitheater for a stunning view. Another summer in Ireland, driving in two small cars, we reached a town after dark and proceeded into a traffic circle—the Irish call them roundabouts—in the *wrong* direction. In an instant the scene resembled electrons scurrying from the nucleus of Uranium 235.

The vacation recorded here was of a different kind. We did not plan a restful interlude. We meant to have a big, crashing good time—to test the proposition that a holiday is beneficial in direct proportion to the degree of change it provides from life's usual routine. As will be seen, events carried the experiment to extremes and prudence would suggest some modifications hereafter. Nevertheless, I favor the general approach. A family group cutting its own trail can have experiences others never know and gather memories worth more than the richest treasures.

This is the story of a holiday packed with challenge and danger. It is an account of what happened to ordinary people and of how they responded to extraordinary events.

Principal Characters

The Americans

	Ages
The Scarsdale Hartzells	
Andrew C. Hartzell	56
Mary Lee Hartzell	52
John M. Hartzell	19
Peter M. Hartzell	17
The Rochester Hartzells	
Thomas C. Hartzell	50
Alice M. Hartzell	49
Linda C. Hartzell	25
Thomas C. Hartzell, Jr. ("Tom Jr.")	23
Roland M. Hartzell	17
Other Relatives	
Ellen McPhillips Baumann	41
Thomas A. Gelwicks ("Tom G.")	31
Stuart C. Law (Honor.) ("Stu")	54

The Africans

Effatta Jonathan	Chief guide
Fred Mtui	1st assistant
Felix Mlotu	2nd assistant
Livingstone and Jasper	Two of the 12 porters
Godfrey Labrosse	Manager, Kibo Hotel

Other Climbers

Keith Moses	American missionary stationed in Kenya
Maria Moses	15
Deborah Moses	14
Alfred Hafner	Swiss climber
Edith Hafner	Swiss climber
Corin Hafner	Swiss climber
Louis DeRooy	Swiss climber
Shigeko Suzuki	Japanese climber
Fujio Tsukada	Japanese climber
Hisao Ishiguro	Japanese climber

The Treacherous Snows

Chapter 1
Fixing the Course

April 15 was my brother Tom's fiftieth birthday. I had once assumed that life would peak long before fifty, and that the journey by that stage would be on the downgrade, slow and dull. But as youth moved with surprising acceleration into adulthood and then middle age, I had found it expedient to exchange my earlier perspective for the more congenial notion that temperament rather than time is the key determinant in how one deals with life and, more importantly, vice versa. There was great satisfaction in seeing this later view exemplified by Tom himself as he completed his fiftieth year. For it was obvious to all that he retained—with the unselfconscious abundance of youth—the energy, affability and courtly good cheer that have always been his distinguishing characteristics and that reflect a wholesome outlook and affirmative disposition. To celebrate the occasion, his wife, Alice, had planned a surprise birthday gathering. Spring being fickle in Rochester, New York, she had royally rescheduled the event for the Memorial Day weekend.

Her skillful maneuvering had diverted Tom from other weekend plans, and he was at home Friday night when, gathered from three states, we appeared. Surprise, greetings, and congratulations followed, and we were soon launched on a sumptuous and sporty suburban weekend.

But families are not always as predictable as they appear. Here, incongruous to the setting and occasion, was a chance to discuss going to the Himalayas. Our son Neil had climbed to the Annapurna base camp a few years earlier; this had set the rest of us talking of a similar adventure. There were imposing obstacles: cost, accommodating Himalayan weather to U.S. school vacations, getting into condition, especially with Tom and me on the lee side of fifty, and fading.

A Himalayan trek brochure appeared mysteriously on the breakfast table Saturday morning. "It's just for conversation," someone said. The men were interested; the women unaccountably cool. After a half hour of casual talk, I heard the word "Christmastime," and, as if by a zoom lens, plans came suddenly into focus. Discussion shifted abruptly from whether we might someday do something exciting to "why not go next Christmas!" Why not, indeed! Real possibilities presented themselves: leave on December 23; go to Midnight Mass on Christmas Eve at Saint Peter's; leave Rome the next day for Kathmandu. It would not be the first time religious fervor launched a great enterprise. Airfare would be steep, and Christmas in Rome would be expensive, but Nepal would be cheap enough. There are no hotel expenses on Annapurna!

Time was a problem; in addition to five or six days for travel, climbing would take at least two weeks. Alice and my wife, Mary Lee, would not climb and were curiously unexcited at waiting fourteen days in Kathmandu.

Another problem was the lack of a clear goal. "What's wrong with hiking a circular route?" I inquired. No one knew, for sure. But the younger men wanted to climb to the *top,* not caring particularly where that might be. Annapurna is 26,000 feet; when first climbed by Herzog in 1950, it was the highest mountain man had conquered. We did not have the experience for that kind of effort. We were amateurs whose objective would not have exceeded the Herzog base camp halfway to the top that Neil had reached. It is no minor matter to get that far; Tom and I would have been satisfied. The others were unconvinced.

We surveyed alternatives at home and abroad. There were great climbs in the West and in the Alps, but it was too late to get organized for the summer. Our son John mentioned Kilimanjaro, which Neil had also climbed. It is 19,340 feet, but because of its location near the equator and geological structure, reaching the top does not, we had been told, require technical skills. It has the further attraction of being near the greatest wild animal range on earth. There were even resorts on the Indian Ocean that the women could visit while we were climbing. Then we could all go on a safari, like normal people. The climb, although reportedly seventy miles round-trip, could be done in five days.

The discussion accelerated. Alice understandably pointed out that she and Tom had already been to Africa—in fact, at Tom's urging they had left the comforts of their tour in Kenya and driven two hundred miles south over dirt roads so, as he explained, "I could make a reconnaissance of the Kilimanjaro area." She noted that it would cost at least $2,000 for each of us to spend the Christmas holidays in the tropical heat, not to mention two consecutive nights in flight getting there. All this to see animals she had met before!

"Why not have Christmas at home and go to the Caribbean in February when the others are back in school," she suggested.

The word "Caribbean" had a strange effect on Mary Lee—I saw her smiling and nodding—and in retrospect, it is hard to deny some merit in their position. But Kilimanjaro was tightening its hold on the rest of us. And while it is often difficult to mark the moment of decision—especially one that turns on subjective urgings rather than on analysis of objective facts—there comes a time when, imperceptibly but apodictically, one knows the decision has

3

been made. The pros and cons may still be debated; objections may be numbered and reviewed, as when a woman lists the deficiencies of a suitor whose proposal she knows she will accept; but the heart realizes the outcome is no longer in doubt. So, at some indeterminate moment that bright spring morning at breakfast, we decided to go.

On Sunday, disagreeable thoughts, like weeds in a garden, began to sprout. Putting estimated costs to paper threatened to spoil the fun. Some present had plans that, as our son Peter said, were "more important than a long trip to climb a lousy mountain." But the rest of us were committed. Tom and I had no trouble. For us, it was now or never. My sister Frances told her son, Tom G., "This is the chance." Mary Lee agreed and said that if no women went, she could spend Christmas with our daughter and her husband in California. Alice, too, was resigned to the foolishness of her husband and sons. She told Mary Lee that one of their neighbors, seeing me in front of the house with Tom, had called to her: "You mean there's another one!"

Tom found slides of their prior trip, including shots of Kilimanjaro and the trail at the start of the climb. The distances were surprising, and the mountain, huge and far-off, intimidating. But the challenge kindled an obstinate defiance, and the thought of sweat and effort was invigorating. What a goal to aim for, what a spur to training, what an awesome prospect! Why should this be left to pictures or books; the action was there for the taking. Of course there would be problems getting organized; there are always obstacles to adventure. An inner timidity whispers, "Why bother?" When you hear that, it's the time to go! The only way is to decide to do it, to start figuring out "how," to discard "whether." When we left for home, it was agreed that I would check airfares and routes. There was no hurry;

4

Christmas was six months away. There could not be that many eccentrics flying to Africa on Christmas Eve.

We discovered that the best route was by KLM overnight to Amsterdam, and then, with stops at Vienna and Khartoum, overnight again to Kilimanjaro Airport, near Moshi, in Tanzania. There was one flight a week from Amsterdam. That meant departing New York December 23, spending Christmas Eve in Amsterdam, and leaving that night to arrive Christmas morning in Africa. Our travel agent reserved thirteen spaces. With ten or more we would get a group rate, and the advantage of being our own "tour." We could climb the first week and then go on safari. This schedule was just right for the climbers, but left open the question of what the others would do while we were on the mountain.

To hold the reservations, we needed a definite commitment for at least ten. I called Tom, who spoke to Alice. She insisted that he and their sons should go without her. Tom G. was definite and so were our sons John and Peter. Then we had an unexpected volunteer: Mary Lee's sister, Ellen, a New York lawyer, heard about our plans and was interested. This was nine. I firmed up all thirteen places, just in case.

In October we went to my thirtieth Yale Law School reunion. There were tables of eight at our class dinner in the elegant President's Room of Woolsey Hall, one of Yale's landmarks. Across from me was Stuart C. Law, a Washington lawyer. He was a Phi Beta Kappa graduate of Yale College, where he had rowed on the Yale crew. We were good friends in law school but I had rarely seen him in the years since graduation. Once was at our twenty-fifth college reunion. He'd then had in tow a young airline stewardess. Stepping ahead of her to shake hands, he said to me, "Be careful, will you, I told Gretchen this was my *fifteenth* reunion." More recently, I had seen him in Washington and was impressed to learn that after a half century as an agnostic, he had became a Catholic and now taught on Sundays at his parish school. He had kept fit over the years, running in marathons and rowing in sculling contests, and I could see that his strength and vigor still matched his forceful personality. Unattached and athletic, he might be both free and interested in Kilimanjaro. Still, I hesitated to ask him on a family expedition.

There were about seventy at the dinner. We went around the tables, each lawyer giving a short talk. The comments were choice blends of affection and humor. Before dinner, a form had been passed around for written comments. George Pratt, a judge on the United States Court of Appeals in New York, read the comment of Bud Blakeley, a former judge in Pennsylvania. Blakeley had written: "I am deeply concerned over the quality of the judiciary, *nationwide.*"

Then it was Samuel Sheats's turn. He was one of three blacks in our class. He had practiced law in Los Angeles and become a judge and arbitrator. This was his first visit to New Haven since graduation. Sam said that when he finished his last exam he was broke and faced the problem of getting to Los Angeles. "Stu Law was driving there, his racing shell on top of his car, and when someone told him I was going, Stu came to my room and offered me a ride. Stu saved me, because I had only twenty dollars to my name."

Stu called out accusingly, "Sam, you told me you were *broke.*"

Sam described their drive across the country and said he had never forgotten that Stu, a conservative Republican WASP from Illinois and "white shoe" graduate of Yale College, with a small crowded car that would have excused taking another passenger, had "sought out a black man to travel with him across the United States. All this was a decade before civil rights became fashionable. We must have made an 'odd couple' in those days."

Then we reached Stu. Echoing the remark that had recently forced the resignation of James Watt as secretary of the interior, he said, "Well, Sam, all we needed was a woman, a Jew, and a cripple to complete the group."

Listening to this happy, poignant exchange, I decided to ask Stu about Kilimanjaro. He was interested, and after giving him a week to reconsider, I telephoned his office and confirmed that he would go. We now had ten.

Because we were our own "tour," I decided to make our own climbing and safari arrangements. With this in mind I visited the Tanzania Tourist Office in New York. The tourist director suggested trip schedules for the climb and the safari and offered to assist us. About that time, however, I received a call from our travel agent, who said that without advance reservations we would squander our time in Africa. I put the matter in his hands. With the Tanzanian tourist director he worked out the program. The men would climb the mountain the first week while Mary Lee and Ellen went to a resort hotel in Zanzibar. Then we would all meet in the town of Arusha and go on to a succession of game lodges.

October 22 was payment day. I telephoned Tom to see if there was any change in his plans. He told me their older daughter Linda had moved back to Rochester, "so she and Alice will go with Mary Lee and Ellen. We're all set."

"Are you sure?" I asked in surprise.

"Absolutely."

"Have you discussed it with them?"

7

"No, not yet . . . but it's definite."

In admiration, I mailed the travel agent a check for twelve round trips to Kilimanjaro.

Chapter 2
Where Is Kilimanjaro?

If you tell a friend you're going to Kilimanjaro, the response will go like this:

"Where *exactly* is Kilimanjaro?"

"In East Africa."

At which point there will be an uncertain pause, because from the ptolemaic perspective of the average American, East Africa is instinctively assumed to be that part closest to the East Coast of the United States. Patronizing pedants, however, will tell you it is on the opposite side, facing the Indian Ocean.

East Africa is a string of countries, running north to south. Without looking at the map, it is hard to get them in retainable mental sequence. Prior to our trip, my mind-map of East Africa was based on leftover impressions from stories of travelers *up* the Nile—especially military travelers, like Gordon, Kitchener, and Winston Churchill—those who journeyed south from Alexandria. I knew there was a vast stretch of Egypt and below it an even larger country, the Sudan. But as to farther south, I was as vague as the early explorers. Although looking at a map removes some of the sport—and one of life's great sports is leaping to a conclusion without verifying facts—one sees that a dogged traveler who continues through Egypt and the Sudan will come eventually, if he survives, to Uganda, and moving south through that benighted land, will finally reach the northern shore of Lake Victoria. If the traveler then persists toward the southeast, across the top of the lake, he will, after a further journey, eventually see rising far ahead the massive summit of Kilimanjaro.

9

The distances are astonishing to Americans, most of whom look east or west and are unsure gauging distances north to south. It is over 2,000 miles up the Nile from Alexandria to Lake Victoria. It is another four hundred miles around the top of the lake and eastward across the African plains to the Tanzanian border near Kilimanjaro. The trip is like a stroll from New York to the Equator, in Brazil.

Lake Victoria and Kenya form most of Tanzania's northern border, and Mozambique most of the southern. The Indian Ocean is on the east; the western border is principally Lake Tanganyika, the longest fresh water lake in the world.

Before World War I, Tanganyika, as it was then called, was part of German East Africa. After the war it became a British colony, and after World War II, a United Nations protectorate. In 1964 it became independent and in 1966 joined with Zanzibar to form the United Republic of Tanzania.

Dar es Salaam, a port on the Indian Ocean, is the capital. The islands of Zanzibar are forty miles northeast. In the coastal areas the heat is oppressive but the higher inland plains, 2,000 to 3,000 feet above sea level, have a pleasant climate.

Although Tanzania is larger than France and Germany combined, it has only 18 million people, most of whom live on the coast. There are enormous inland plains for the great array of wild animals.

Ninety-nine percent of the people are black. About 31 percent are Moslems and an equal number, Christians. Swahili and English are the principal languages but the literacy rate is only 66 percent. The population is still largely divided into tribes which inhabit their own areas. The eastern and southern approaches to Kilimanjaro are populated by the Chagga tribe; adjacent and to the west are the famous Masai, once the most fierce and today the most photographed of black Africans.

Although it is only two hundred miles from the coast, no European saw Kilimanjaro until 1848. Like many other great natural wonders, its discovery was the serendipitous bonus of the missionary's quest for converts. Johannes Rebmann and Ludwig Krapf, two young Germans, were members of the Church Missionary Society, whose headquarters were in London. They were stationed on the coast at Rabbai Mpia, directly east of Kilimanjaro and near present-day Mombasa, in Kenya. The coastal natives, who were principally Moslems, resisted conversion and the missionaries may have hoped for more success inland. They decided to establish a chain of mission stations extending 1,000 miles across Africa to the Atlantic. Their ambition matched that of the Franciscans who, one hundred years earlier, had built missions, each a day's march from the other, up the coast of California. To prepare for their project, Rebmann and Krapf made exploratory treks inland. On the second of those Krapf was left behind ill, but Rebmann set off near the end of April 1848, toward a region the natives called Jagga, where there were reported to be high country and mountains. The area was inhabited by the Chagga Tribe, and the higher land promised a good climate for the first station.

For twelve days Rebmann moved west. On the morning of May 10 he saw an enormous mountain, its summit in a cloud of white. A few moments later, he realized that the cloud was snow. Rebmann published an account of his discovery in England the following year but many scoffed at his report. English geographers were then busy speculating about the sources of the Nile, the location of which had proved to be one of history's most elusive geographical facts. Some argued those sources would be found in central Africa, while others believed they were farther east. Rebmann's description of Kilimanjaro, particularly his claim that, despite its location just below the Equator, its top was covered with snow—which suggested a very high mountain—was for some participants in the debate an unsettling observation they wanted to omit from the geographic equation. For that reason, his report was dismissed or ignored by those who believed the Nile's sources were further west.

Thirteen years later, however, Baron K. K. Von der Becken, a German aristocrat, confirmed Rebmann's account. Von der Becken tried to climb Kilimanjaro in 1861 and again in 1862, but failed. It was not until a quarter century later, in 1889, that Hans Meyer, a German geologist, reached the summit on his second attempt. Since that time the climb has become a major attraction. Kilimanjaro is one of the highest mountains in the world that can be conquered without technical skill. It requires only stamina fueled, say some, by stupidity.

Kilimanjaro's majestic summit rises alone, gigantic and unchallenged, out of the African plain. Unlike virtually every other major mountain, it has no rivals and from a distance it seems to be separate from the earth itself. English geologists have determined that it was produced by volcanic eruptions that formed the East African Rift Valley, which is part of a larger phenomenon called the Great Rift Valley. The latter is a 6,000-mile crack in the Earth's crust, stretching from Lebanon to Mozambique. The rift varies in size but is generally thirty miles across and in certain parts of Africa plainly appears as a dip in the earth. Subterranean forces once tore the Earth's crust apart, causing the land in between to sink down. The same pressures forced up molten rock in volcanic eruptions, some of which are still going on in a few of the volcanos that border the rift. Kilimanjaro, which is one hundred miles east of where the rift passes through Tanzania, is no longer considered an active volcano. The Olduvai Gorge, site of the great anthropological discoveries, is directly west of Kilimanjaro and almost in the center of the rift in Tanzania.

The Kilimanjaro massif extends in an east-west direction for fifty miles and comprises three principal volcanos. On the east is Mawenzi, a 17,564-foot peak; seven miles to the west is Kibo, the peak popularly referred to as Kilimanjaro. Farther west is the Shira Ridge, which rises to 13,140 feet and is the remnant of an earlier crater. Mawenzi is a jagged peak, formed by the stripping off of what was once a volcanic crater. Kibo, which lies across a desert-like "saddle" from Mawenzi, has a circular summit, the top of a crater one and a half miles across. Glacial ice covers portions of the Kibo cone, and freezing rain and snow occur during the wet seasons, which are the spring and fall.

Because it is only three degrees below the equator, the approaches to Kilimanjaro, at 3,000 to 5,000 feet, have tropical vegetation. Higher up, there are several altitudinal zones. A climber goes from a tropical region at the start all the way to arctic conditions at the top. Near the summit, temperatures can vary, between midday and midnight, by 70 degrees.

On the southern slopes the Chagga people raise bananas, coffee, and vegetables. Farther up there is a rain forest and, still higher, open scrubland. Here one finds the giant lobelias and groundsels. The lobelias are plants that look like green-shrouded gnomes, sullen and unattractive. The groundsels are weedlike plants that in the ultraviolet rays of high altitudes grow to heights of thirty feet. They too are weird in form and texture, with woody palm-tree type trunks and two or three large limbs, at the top of which are great bursts of cabbage-like leaves.

Kilimanjaro is the world's fifty-first highest mountain. It is nearly 6,000 feet higher than the Grand Teton (13,740 feet) and almost 5,000 feet higher than the Matterhorn (14,692 feet). The frozen carcass of the world's most famous leopard was found on the crater rim in 1926. Despite Hemingway's dour comment about no one explaining what the leopard was seeking at that altitude, scholars suggest that the leopard must have been prowling the mountain in search of the rodents and hydraxes that sneak out of the rocks at night to feast on the giant lobelia leaves. In 1961 a group of wild dogs, perhaps on a similar hunt, was seen on the Kibo rim.

For all these reasons, Kilimanjaro is a mountain of extraordinary interest. If one scoured the earth, it would be hard to find a more exciting, and at the same time manageable, challenge.

Chapter 3
The Lure of the Climb

Whatever its exotic attraction, why go 11,000 miles to climb any mountain? We wondered ourselves at this interest, which developed almost by chance over the years.

We started hiking in New Hampshire's White Mountains in the 1960s. These were strenuous but civilized climbs—although the Huntington Ravine Trail on Mount Washington can have early morning ice, even in August. A few hours on these trails brings one above the tree line, with views unmatched east of the Rockies. These climbs were stored in a backpack of happy memories and have often been drawn out for comparison when others have described their adventures.

One summer we were in London. On an early morning run in Kensington Gardens, I came upon a stone obelisk with these chiseled words:

In Memory of
SPEKE
Victoria Nyanza
And the Nile
1864

The weathered sentinel, alone amidst the summer green, with its strange message, made a sharp impression. I knew of Speke and the other explorers of East Africa. They were men who had left the comforts of Victorian England for a dark and dangerous land. Perhaps they were spurred by the missionary's zeal, or by the hope of acclaim in this world or the next. But there must have been something more. It could have been that buoyancy that comes with

15

relying on oneself far from help and safety. Admiration and a trace of envy stayed with me. They were small catalysts, years later, in the decision to go.

Another summer we climbed Pike's Peak in Colorado. This is a tough one-day hike. There is a restaurant at the top—the highest in the United States—for those who drive up the automobile road or take the cog railway. It is a special reward for the few who get there on foot. An hour up the trail we met a man in his sixties, descending slowly. He had started up the previous day, tagging behind those who had run the Pike's Peak marathon, possibly the world's most awesome race. He had reached the top in late afternoon, but on his return darkness had caught him on steep switchbacks a thousand feet below the summit. Wisely he had huddled down on the narrow trail through the night, waiting for daybreak. By the time we saw him he was warm and cheerful in the morning sun. Hearing his story, I was sure his high spirits arose more from the satisfaction of knowing he had used good judgment than from his present safety and comfort. We gave him some food to hold him until he reached the trailhead below. On we continued, reaching a ranger cabin at 11,000 feet. Our daughter Lee was flushed and was having blurred vision and seeing double. She prudently decided to turn back. The weather was ideal and there were other hikers coming down, so we let her return alone. We continued to the summit, where I was nauseous. Lying on a bench did not help. We hitched a ride down and I felt fine as we reached the lower levels. This was my first experience with the effects of high altitude. I had been on Pike's Peak before, but had gone up on the railway and had felt normal. The hike demonstrated how exertion at altitude takes its toll and that the trouble once started is not necessarily corrected by resting.

A week later, we climbed Mount Whitney in California. At 14,495 feet, it is the highest United States peak outside Alaska, and a far more rugged climb than Pike's Peak. The round trip is twenty-one miles and normally takes two days; there are no roads on the mountain and only a stone shed, full of snow, at the top. On the first day we made it to a barren area of flat rocks with a pool of water at 12,000 feet; the maps invitingly call this moonscape "Trail Camp"—it is an excellent place to give up. After a wretched night, when we slept poorly for lack of oxygen and shivered for lack of warm sleeping bags, we started early, reaching the top at 1:00 P.M. The panorama on this highest point of the Sierras is extraordinary whether one looks east or west. We ate peanut butter and jelly sandwiches, but I had trouble swallowing the dry bread.

As we started down, the increasing oxygen could be felt. Half a mile below the summit, we met a man of about seventy coming up. An even older woman was behind him, and, still farther back, a couple in their twenties. This Sierra version of John the Baptist—he had a staff, naturally—immediately launched into a sermon on the health habits of the old woman, pointing back and announcing she was seventy-seven and climbed to the top each year. Shaking his arms and assuming we couldn't make the calculation, he stated that if she did the climb in three years—as she certainly intended—she would be eighty. He then gave us details about her diet, listing her favorite vegetables and emphasizing that, although a vegetarian, we should be aware she consumed fish and eggs. We nodded our vigorous approval.

This part of the exhortation was barely complete before the vegetarian reached us. We gave her our most courteous "Hello," inadequate though we sensed it would be. She was not one to squander time on amenities, however, and asked at once whether we had been to church that morning, it being Sunday. I started to say we regretted not having seen her there, but fearing she might knock me off the slope, which was here quite steep, I settled for obsequiously explaining that we did go every Sunday except under the most unusual circumstances, venturing the hope she might deem the present one to qualify. She gave us the pitying look one reserves for derelicts but did not pursue the subject. Instead she returned to her diet, our souls presumably being of secondary importance, although the point seemed to be that the right attention to diet would save one's soul.

As this second part of the sermon proceeded, the Baptist, unable to keep silent, interjected that keeping fit would also enable us to climb the mountain as vigorously as she did. The younger couple, smiling like sheep, said nothing. Then "the venerables" turned, and with annoying ease continued up the rocks toward the summit. We often mused about this encounter. They were indeed extraordinary specimens and showed what was possible for those in good condition.

Several years later, we returned to Mount Whitney. To my astonishment, we met the vegetarian again, this time at Trail Camp, where she and a retinue of admirers were acclimatizing themselves for the top. She was eighty-three, and had apparently outlasted the Baptist, who was not present. But she was still at it and, with her younger friends, now had pamphlets espousing both God and exercise. Nearby, looking poorly, was a TV camera crew. They had dragged themselves and their equipment to record our friend "on location" for a TV program. As I was trying to start a breakfast fire early the next morning, I saw her stride by like a majorette, her followers in the rear. I never saw her again—probably because I wore out a mile below the summit and found resting such an exquisite pleasure that I gave up. Although not appreciating it at the time, having to stop on this climb taught me another lesson in pacing myself at high altitudes.

The average hiker rarely feels the need to ponder why, physically and psychologically, climbing is fun. It is enough that it is, and everyone is instinctively aware of the lift provided by exercise, fresh air and unusual vistas. But it can be pointed out that a climb is more invigorating than a walk. One is going *up,* not just over. Climbing works up a sweat faster, like a run. It usually lasts much longer and, if the pace is right, one feels better at the end of the day, even if tired, than at the start. One can see more of the route when hiking than when riding, flying, or running. In the drier air at high altitudes objects are clearer and sharper, because there is less moisture to look through. There is time to take it all in. At increasing elevations, there are trees first, then shrubs, and finally only rock. The higher up, the wider the view; the climber gets the bird's perspective and the satisfaction of accomplishment.

I once heard a speaker describe the opportunities and the risks of a Harvard education. He said the student should not settle for what is packaged and presented, important as that may be. He provided the example of a nineteenth-century Harvard president who, in addition to his formal duties, found time each day to sit in his garden observing a resident frog. He recorded in a notebook how often the frog opened its jaws to snap up bugs and which bugs it ate. After days of surveillance, he had a record of how many flies, moths, and water bugs the frog consumed per hour, of how its intake related to its size, and of other anuran particulars. By direct observation, he had educated himself in the eating habits of a frog. No one had collected and delivered the information to him. Although the president of the nation's second greatest university, he had not let formal education blunt his mental initiative in educating himself.

As a chance for self-education, a mountain hike beats frog watching by quite a pace. One observes directly and there is time to wonder. Nature at close range invites inquiry about cause and effect; there can be moments when one achieves a sudden, and for oneself original, Darwinian synthesis. At the same time, one is absorbed in monitoring one's body and its response to the demands put upon it. Each major climb can be a "course" in itself.

Chapter 4
Oxygen and Altitude

No one should climb high without (a) being in shape, (b) understanding the effects of altitude on the body, and (c) thoroughly knowing the route. My first objective was to trim down, keeping in mind that every extra pound would have to be carried to a height where the air had less than half the oxygen of air at sea level. This meant regular and longer runs and a steady increase in stretches, sit-ups, and push-ups. I added fifty knee bends a day to my other exercises, aware that the final mile up Kilimanjaro was very steep. Slowly, as fall slipped into winter, my weight fell and my stamina and strength increased. By mid-December I was in better condition than at any time since my youth. On December 23, an hour before we left for the airport, I took a final seven-mile run, smugly pleased that, while still earning a living, I had pushed my conditioning to a reasonable limit.

There was also the need to learn the secrets of climbing in thin air. I found the perfect book: *Going High—The Story of Man and Altitude,* by Charles S. Houston, M.D.* Dr. Houston has spent years studying the effects of altitude and is among the world's leading authorities. His book, which anyone will find informative and which is indispensable for high climbers, explains the chemical and physiological reactions to hiking in thin air. From this book and other sources, I gained the following understanding—al-

*Published by Charles S. Houston, M.D., The American Alpine Club (New York: 1980).

though I hasten to add the caution that no one whose life may depend on it should rely solely on this explanation.

We are all taught but have little need to remember that we live under a weight of air, and that air like water will rush into every vacuum. Breathing out creates a vacuum, and atmospheric pressure forces air into the nose and mouth, down the trachea and into the bronchial tubes which decrease in size until they end in tiny air sacks called alveoli. As it moves through the trachea and into the lungs, air is continuously saturated with water, warmed and cleaned. Exercise increases the rush of air, requiring extra body water and heat to moisten and warm it. This is especially true in the cold dry air of higher altitudes, which is why hikers must be sure to consume great quantities of water. As we later noticed, signs at the Kilimanjaro huts advised hikers to drink at least eight quarts of liquid a day. We found this impossible, although we supplemented our water intake with large quantities of soup and tea.

The air that enters the body loses some of its force as it works its way down to the alveoli. From these tiny sacs it passes into the capillaries, which flow through the alveoli and carry the red blood cells that, like a passenger ferry, pick up and transport oxygen. At this point also carbon dioxide from the blood, moving in the opposite direction, passes from the capillaries into the alveoli, to be carried to the outside when one exhales.

This alveoli–capillary transfer point must always be free of obstacles. Any interference with the transfer, such as thickening of the alveoli or capillary walls, or a squeez-ing-off or enlargement of the alveoli, as in emphysema, means that less oxygen crosses through for pickup by the blood cells. Fluid in the alveoli creates the same problem. High climbers must, at their peril, understand this fact.

The heart is the engine that powers the oxygen-carrying blood. It works in three stages. First, the heart muscles relax, and the veins pour blood into the right ventricle. Then the heart muscles contract, pumping the blood from the right ventricle through the alveoli of the lungs for the discharge of carbon dioxide and the pickup of oxygen, after which the blood flows back into the left ventricle. Then the heart contracts again and the left ventricle pumps the oxygenated blood into the arteries. When the heart relaxes, the arterial blood, having delivered its oxygen to the tissues and picked up carbon dioxide in exchange, flows back through the veins to the right ventricle, completing the cycle.

Blood transports oxygen because the red cells have a molecule called hemoglobin which takes on oxygen. Hemoglobin contains, among other things, four atoms of heme or iron. Oxygen seats itself on the iron atoms which also accommodate nitrate, forming another molecule which gives a bluish color to a person's nails and lips if there is not enough oxygen present. Some people, especially blacks, have mutant forms of hemoglobin, including the S form, which is not as good for seating oxygen. This can produce anemia. Dr. Houston recommends that a black person who plans to climb above 10,000 or 12,000 feet should be checked to ensure that his hemoglobin does not leave him susceptible to altitude sickness. Ironically, all the guides and porters on Kilimanjaro are black.

It is also important not to climb high within three months after donating blood. The normal red blood cell count is 44 percent of blood volume. The Sherpas of Nepal and others who live at high altitudes may have 50–55 percent. Donating a pint of blood reduces the red blood cell count from 44 percent to 40 percent, or by 10 percent (there are about ten pints of blood in the body). Although blood volume is restored in a healthy person in twenty-four hours, the red blood cell count builds back up only at the rate of 1 percent per day of what was lost. This means it takes one hundred days to get back to normal, which is why institutions do not take blood donations from a person more often than every three to four months.

There are fifteen grams of hemoglobin in each one hundred milliliters of blood. This quantity of hemoglobin, if the "seats" are fully occupied, will accommodate twenty milliliters of oxygen. If the oxygen content of air is low, there will be empty "seats" because not enough oxygen will have boarded as the red blood cells pass through the alveoli. However, reduction in oxygen can be partially compensated by an increase in hemoglobin, as if more empty seats caused a surge in the boarding process. This occurs naturally when the body adapts to altitude. Although the adaptive process begins after even one day in thinner air, a significant increase in the hemoglobin count can require many weeks. Dr. Houston believes that adaptation has been given more credit than it deserves because, as the amount of hemoglobin increases, so does the viscosity of the blood; and if the blood is too thick, the red cells may bunch up, decreasing their ability to seat oxygen and later release it to the tissues.

The acidity of the blood also affects the movement of oxygen into the blood. Carbon dioxide, in its opposite movement from the blood to the alveoli, accelerates the transfer of oxygen into the blood. Most of the carbon dioxide in the body, however, dissolves in the plasma or liquid portion of the blood, forming a weak acid. If carbon dioxide is decreased by overbreathing, which often happens at high altitudes, the loss of acidity in the blood and the increase in alkalinity impairs the oxygen movement. There is one drug that seems to help prevent the loss of carbon dioxide and hence assists in maintaining the correct acidity; it is acetazolamide or Diamox. As mentioned later, we took Diamox the fourth night on Kilimanjaro and it may have improved our short sleep just before we started for the summit.

The vital last step in the oxygen transport system is the release of arterial oxygen to the tissues. A chilled body impedes this release. This accounts for the sluggishness characteristic of hypothermia at high altitudes. A climber must therefore be warmly dressed for the cold of higher altitudes, because warmth is critical to strength and coordination.

No one should hike above 9,000 feet without understanding the process of respiration. The details, however, may be hard to recall in the excitement of a mountain crisis. This problem can be anticipated by a diagram of the oxygen and carbon dioxide transport system, with underscoring of potential trouble points, and by a list of the symptoms which warn of trouble. Both should be carried with the first aid kit, and easily accessible. Each hiker will then have at hand a diagram of how the body maintains "homeostasis," that is, constancy of internal condition, despite changes in its outward surroundings. This is the essential process of all living beings. The late Hans Selye, M.D., in his classic work, *The Stress of Life,* provides a lucid explanation of the subject.* His statement at the front of his book is particularly pertinent to mountain climbers: "This book is dedicated to those who are not afraid to enjoy the stress of a full life, nor so naive as to think that they can do so without intellectual effort."

Understanding the body's respiratory functions is es-

*Hans Selye, M.D., *The Stress of Life,* rev. ed. (New York: McGraw-Hill, 1978).

sential for comprehending the three general forms of altitude sickness: acute mountain sickness, high altitude pulmonary edema, and high altitude cerebral edema. I knew from my prior climbs that most of us would suffer in some degree from acute mountain sickness.

This discomfort, which is generally triggered by hiking too fast to 8,000 or 10,000 feet, is characterized primarily by nausea and occasional vomiting. One also has an atypical headache, which feels more like the flu than a bona fide sea-level headache. At times, there can be shortness of breath, but I have never been able to distinguish it from "regular" shortness of breath at high altitudes. Eating requires effort and some swallows—particularly of bread and other dry food—are hard to get down. Sleeping is possible but unpleasant. Such a list of symptoms, however, overstates the total feeling. One is not incapacitated and can still enjoy life. And I have never seen anyone with these symptoms who had, more than usual, difficulty in thinking. So the illness, while discomforting, is generally not serious and one need not give up and descend. It is usually self-limiting and corrects itself if one proceeds slowly.

Pulmonary edema, which I had never seen first-hand prior to Kilimanjaro, is far more serious and, although a reader will find it hard to accept the fact, can quickly be fatal. It results from fluid accumulating in the lungs and impeding the oxygen–carbon dioxide transfer. How altitude and lack of oxygen cause this accumulation is not fully understood. Possibly the increased blood pressure in the pulmonary artery at higher altitudes squeezes fluid out of the blood more rapidly than it can be absorbed. The result, whatever its precise mechanism, is a slow accumulation in the interstices between the alveoli and the capillaries. After a day or two, the accumulation seeps into the alveoli itself. The oxygen–carbon dioxide transfer is hindered, and the condition worsens rapidly, causing serious illness and, if corrective action is not promptly taken, death. The symptoms vary: excessive shortness of breath, unusual fatigue, a slight fever, and—the most telltale signs—a crackling cough, caused by the fluid, and a bloody spit.

Another symptom is cyanosis, the blue cast that results from a lack of oxygenated hemoglobin. This is a tricky condition, and I was not sufficiently alert to it. A person deficient in hemoglobin may also be deficient in oxygen because there is not enough hemoglobin to seat the oxygen. But unless the person has *very* deficient oxygen, the blue danger signal will not appear because there is enough oxygen for the deficient supply of hemoglobin. A person with a normal amount of hemoglobin but insufficient oxygen will quickly exhibit cyanosis. A blue cast, therefore, which may appear at the base of the lips or in the whole face, flags a serious problem when seen on a mountain.

There is a vivid description of pulmonary edema in *Mountaineering, The Freedom on the Hills** at page 439:

> Pulmonary Edema is the leakage of blood plasma into the lungs, which renders the air sacs (alveoli) ineffective in exchanging oxygen and carbon dioxide in the blood . . . The early symptoms . . . are that of pneumonia. Within twelve to thirty-six hours after reaching high altitude the victim . . . experiences extreme weakness, shortness of breath, nausea, vomiting, very rapid pulse (120-160), Cyanosis (bluish color), "noisy" breathing which progresses to moist crackling breath sounds and irritated coughing which produces a frothy white or pink sputum and later blood.
>
> If untreated, the victim rapidly moves into the final

The Mountaineers, 4th ed. (Seattle, Washington: 1982).

phase characterized by unconsciousness and bubbles in the mouth and nose. If the unconscious victim is not immediately moved to lower elevation or given oxygen, he will die. All the early symptoms may be mistaken for "Mountain Sickness" or fatigue, or may pass unnoticed during the night, with the morning finding the victim unconscious and in the final phase. The most effective first aid is rapid evacuation to lower altitude or a constant administration of oxygen.

This was the major and indeed only real risk I foresaw as we prepared for Kilimanjaro. I was aware of the distinction between acute mountain sickness, which I had already experienced and seen in others, and pulmonary edema. I was alert to the need to watch myself and the others for any gurgling cough or bloody spit.

Strangely, I paid less attention to the danger of cerebral edema, which is caused by fluid in the brain and is even more serious than fluid in the lungs. This usually happens at higher altitudes than pulmonary edema but nevertheless can occur above 12,000 feet. Why I did not have this problem as much in mind I cannot, in retrospect, explain. Of course, as a matter of common sense, I knew that any lack of motor coordination by myself or others meant trouble. But I did not know that persistent double vision from weak or oxygen-deprived eye muscles could be a warning sign of this condition. Nor did I fully appreciate that cerebral edema can deceptively interfere with judgment and with auditory functions.

Either type of edema, therefore, demands immediate descent regardless of whether it is day or night, regardless of weather, regardless of anyone's plea for rest. Getting down is the only solution, and there is literally no time to spare because the sick person not only needs oxygen but also the atmospheric pressure of a lower altitude, to drive the oxygen through an impaired respiratory system into the tissues.

Before we left, I telephoned Dr. Houston and explained our plans, telling him our ages and describing our conditions. I asked whether we were stupid to attempt Kilimanjaro. Because none of us had heart or lung problems, he said we were not too rash. He emphasized that we should go slow and recommended more than the scheduled five days. "Extra time on the way up," he said, "is more important than condition. It is also important to carry as little as possible and drink lots of water." I asked what we should look for as indicating pulmonary edema. He told me excessive shortness of breath, blood in the sputum, coughing with a gurgling sound in the chest. "Watch your companions and yourself. If someone has any of these signs, turn back immediately. Don't just rest, assuming the condition will improve; getting down will alone save you." He said a friend of his had been part of a group on Kilimanjaro, several of whom, feeling bad, wanted to rest. They were approaching the top but were too tired to go on. The friend roused them and made them start down, realizing that if they rested they might die. Despite this sobering advice, Dr. Houston was basically affirmative. I felt, medically speaking, we had done all we could and that, although there was some risk, it was prudent to go ahead.

We also needed to learn about the route. Neil explained each day's hike and we studied his pictures. He mentioned the guides' constant admonition, *"Poli, poli"* ("slowly," in Swahili), the headache and nausea he had the third night at 15,500 feet, and the cold of the summit. He had climbed at the same time of year, shortly after Christmas. The weather was dry and, although there is glacial snow on the summit cone, the route he had followed was over volcanic rock, called scree, which, after the end of the fall rains, is clear of snow. There was the problem of sliding back a little after each step in the scree; this is discouraging and exhausting, but not dangerous. To avoid it, climbers begin their final push at 1:00 A.M., when the scree is frozen.

I read six accounts of other climbs, several of which had also been made in late December or January. They gave details of the route and of the equipment required. The first day's hike was ten miles to 9,500 feet; the second day, eleven miles, to 12,500 feet; the third day, eleven miles to 15,500 feet, and the fourth night, three and a half miles to 18,635 feet, at Gillman's Point on the southeastern rim of the summit cone. (These distances, however, were overstated; figures on a Tanzania government map show the route as a third shorter.) From Gillman's Point, it is possible to go around the rim which rises another 705 feet to 19,340 at Uruhu Peak, the highest point. Gillman's Point, however, is considered the summit and those who get there receive—when they return to the bottom—a certificate from the Tanzania National Park. I felt Gillman's Point would be enough for me, although some of the others were aiming for Uruhu.

In addition to all the obvious items of hiking and cold weather gear, we took compasses, thermometers attached to some jackets, sun hats and lotion (ultraviolet rays increase 10 percent for every 1,000 feet of elevation), Chapsticks, face masks, sunglasses or goggles, rope and water-purification tablets. Most important of all, we had aluminum emergency blankets in palm-size packets which, when unfolded, are remarkably warm and can be life-saving if one is injured or trapped on a mountain. We also had emergency rations of dry peanuts, raisins, and granola bars.

Chapter 5
To Amsterdam

As December sped along, I relished the prospect that twelve of us would shove all obstacles aside and converge at Kennedy Airport on the unlikely evening of December 23. A note from Ellen, sent to my office with her check for some final expenses, hinted at the effort:

> Here it is, with the hope that I really will make that plane tomorrow night.

The advance guard was Tom G., who arrived at our doorstep two days early, fully equipped. A thirty-one-year-old bachelor lawyer from Cincinnati, he had for some time been pointed to by friends at home as "preparing for Kilimanjaro." Fit and with a new protective beard, he sported a blue Gore-Tex windjacket, a gift from his girlfriend that was to make him the sartorial standout among us.

Stu, although he did not have far to come, took equal care against weather and Christmas traffic. He arrived in New York a day early and spent the night with friends in the city. Stu had promised to appear in the "outfit I wore with Hillary thirty years ago," but he appeared at Kennedy accoutered—contrary to our rules—in a shirt, tie, and sport coat. When challenged, he said, "I meant at the queen's reception for Hillary." Charged with being over-dressed, he countered by revealing that his tie was only a clip-on, which he promptly removed.

In South Bend, Indiana, the previous morning had been dark and cold. Tom Jr. struggled awake in his dorm at Notre Dame Law School. Three "all nighters" during exam week had taken their toll. His digital clock showed 8:28 A.M. He stared at it blankly for some moments before realizing that he was not going to make an 8:42 flight. Desperately hoping the plane was delayed, he called the airport, only to learn the plane would leave on time. He rushed down the hall, looking for someone who might race him to the airport. The hall was deserted. Missing the plane would have a chain-reaction effect because the Rochester Hartzells had planned to meet him at noon and leave for Scarsdale.

Pressing for alternatives, he got space on a later flight, which, with a change of planes in Cleveland, would reach Rochester at 2:00 P.M.. This flight was delayed, and he missed the connection in Cleveland. On still another flight—jammed with Christmas travelers—he finally arrived at 5:00. Linda met him and they rushed downtown where, although past office hours, his doctor waited with a gamma globulin shot. Finally, at 7:30, he and his family were on the road.

We spent our last morning getting final items and checking gear. Ellen called from the office to say she would finish just in time to get home and then to the airport. Stu confirmed that he was ready for launch. The Rochester Hartzells arrived at 3:00 P.M., having driven through a blizzard and spent the night enroute. At 4:00 we assembled for quiche and drinks and at 5:00 left for the airport.

Hauling out our packs at Kennedy, I gazed wonderingly as Tom lifted suitcases and his attache case from the trunk of his car. All the others soon arrived. Ellen wore a safari coat and she and Mary Lee each had a single carry-on bag and no other luggage.

Our departure was delayed an hour, so we found our way to the second-floor restaurant in the center of the International Building, settling down in a comfortable lounge with drinks. Soon the men drifted to the buffet line for dinner. The meat carver, a hearty black fellow in white clothes and chef's hat, made faces at the back of a customer who asked to have his roast beef topped with grated cheese. The carver wanted to know where we were heading and when Tom Jr. told him, said with a grin: "Say hi to my brothers." Then he called after us, "Good luck on the mountain."

In the spacious KLM 747 we were seated across the width of the plane. After we reached cruising altitude and were about to be served another dinner, I heard Tom, who was seated on the opposite side, explaining to the steward that I, rather than he, was "Mr. Andrew Hartzell."

The steward then came around and presented me with a bottle of champagne, "with the compliments of Mr. van den Assum." I did not know the name and am regrettably unaccustomed to such special attention—although well disposed toward it. The steward knew no more than I who our welcome benefactor was, but he showed me a letter to KLM officials at Kennedy requesting the bottle for me. My law firm represents KLM in the United States. Someone there must have heard of our trip and decided on this elegant gesture. We passed the bottle around, with cheerful toasts.

Most long flights are for reading, the movie, or sleep. Tonight was different. I was not sleepy, despite the day's preparations and the afternoon run, which sometimes catches up to me by midevening. It was such a relief to have pulled out of the Christmas rush, to have all twelve of us together and happily on our way, that these were indeed special hours. There was no need, as there always seems to be, to make every minute "count." Talking to Mary Lee, and occasionally with one of the others, I did not sleep at all. It seemed only a short time before a strip of dull light appeared ahead, quickly widening into morning. We crossed the line of the Irish coast, green even in December. Soon it was time for breakfast. Then I looked down over England. At 10:45 A.M. Dutch time we landed in Amsterdam.

KLM had a group of pretty, uniformed attendants at a counter as we entered the terminal. They told us in perfect English where we could check our bags for the day and get a shuttle bus to the Hotel Ibis, which is next to the airport, and where we had had the foresight to reserve rooms for washing-up and resting. The day was mild but gray, and the flat Dutch countryside colorless. But Christmas Eve casts its own spell.

The hotel was an uninspiring modern structure, like airport hotels everywhere, but with the undeniable charm of proximity and beds. We had six adjacent rooms along a narrow corridor. These were a gift from our travel agent. They were at ground level, and looked out into the wide countryside. Most of our group headed for bed, but Mary Lee, Ellen, and I wanted to see Amsterdam, and especially the house of Anne Frank. We discovered that a bus for the center of town would soon be leaving. The ride took half an hour and we were the only passengers, although the bus appeared to be on a regular route.

As we approached the center of Amsterdam, the houses became increasingly picturesque. Many had gabled roofs that leaned out toward the street; others had elaborate balconies. The windows were tall and stately, and often the most distinctive feature. The closer to the center of town, the older and more individual the houses became. Many were centuries old.

A series of canals, like concentric moats, encircle the center of Amsterdam, the outer half of the crescent disappearing into the harbor. Houses face the canals, which serve as boulevards. Most of the houses are tall, with three or four high-ceilinged floors, and many are several rooms deep. In the earlier days the houses were also workshops and warehouses—many still are—and supplies and finished products are carried by barges on the canals. The signs of this activity are apparent in the extensions with hoists at second and third floor openings.

We left the bus at Dam Square, in the heart of the city. The streets and shops were sparsely decorated, considering it was Christmas Eve, because the Dutch celebrate more the feast of Saint Nicholas, on December 6. Seeking directions to the Anne Frank house, we were surprised at the quick comprehension of those we asked. Each understood us immediately and gave us clear directions, although we managed to make a few wrong turns and had to inquire three times. I have often asked directions in London and been required to repeat myself to Englishmen straining to translate my American. Not the Amsterdam Dutch. They seem to find it routine.

The Anne Frank house is a tall row house with high-ceilinged rooms above the ground level. It stands in the center of a block of similar well-proportioned, distinctive stone buildings, all facing a tree-lined cobblestone street that serves as the strand of the Prinsengracht Canal. The houses, the street, and the canal give the impression of business mixed with graceful living. Except for two flags on either side of the first floor there is nothing to distinguish No. 263 from the other houses until one is directly in front. There, engraved on a metal plaque on the stone wall are the words, "Anne Frank *Huis*."

The ground floor was once a store and warehouse, at the back of which spices were manufactured. In the years before World War II, the business was managed by Otto Frank, Anne's father. Outside steps lead to the first floor, which, in the Franks' time, contained the company offices. The large front room is today the ticket room, and except for a few wooden chairs it is bare, with nothing to distract one's thoughts from the grim events that took place there. Behind the ticket room are other large rooms which were also offices and, farther back and up a few steps, another former office and kitchen. At the left of the front room, steps lead to a small second floor landing, with doors on the right and left. The left leads to storerooms at the front. The right, as ordinary as the door of a closet, opens to narrow steep steps to the *Het Achterhuis*—"the house behind." This was the secret annex where the Frank family hid. Shortly after they went into the building, one of Otto Frank's co-workers disguised the door by building a bookcase on the side facing the landing. Today the bookcase door is pulled back, and visitors can climb to the floor above.

At the top of the stairs there are two sizable rooms. One was the parents' bedroom; Anne shared the other with her sister. The windows of both rooms overlook the rear gardens and garages of other houses which enclose the large rectangular block. On the right is a small room with a wash basin and toilet. Another stairway leads to the third floor and opens into a large bright room, its windows also facing the back. There is a sink and stove, the room originally having been a laboratory for the spice company. This was the living room, dining room and scullery for the stowaways. Perhaps because they are not strange surroundings but, indeed, are similar to rooms in many homes, I felt immediately the presence of those who here—not so long ago—endured months and then years, waiting and hoping. Pictures, taken at the time, show the room just as it is today.

One wall has a map of France and the Low Countries. Drawn on it, the dates penned in, are the lines of advance of the Allied Armies in the weeks after D-day. The lines open slowly south from Normandy, stubbornly refusing through July to turn east toward Holland. One can still sense the hopes of those who made this anxious record.

Although the living room looks reasonably comfortable, the hideaways lived in constant fear of discovery. The big rear windows were partly blocked by green slats to prevent detection from below. Pieces of the slats are still attached to the window frames. Movements were quiet and no one could run water or use the toilet during working hours.

On the floor below, Anne's bedroom still has on the walls magazine pictures of American movie stars—Dianna Durbin, Ginger Rogers, Clark Gable and Rita Hayworth—evidence of the young girl's effort to find, in their glamorous smiles, the reflection of a brighter life. Unlike the rest of us, who have been showered with the blessings of freedom, this was to be her only escape.

On the first floor, there is a front room with a display of Frank family photographs, taken before and during the years of hiding. There are also letters and papers by Anne. One can follow her from babyhood until her first high school year. In the pictures she looks out with a shy smile. No wonder this is the most famous house in Amsterdam.

Chapter 6
Africa

Amsterdam airport on Christmas Eve was a scene of bustle and cheer. We arrived with time to spare and descended on the attractive shops that stretch the length of the large terminal. At 7:45 the flashing departure screen signalled us to the plane. There the gate area was filled and the flight appeared fully booked. I saw a few other Americans going on safari, and some blacks, presumably returning home, but most of the passengers were Europeans in normal attire, which seemed unusual for a once-a-week flight to Africa. The plane was a stretch DC-8 and more confining than our 747. But it was clean, well-appointed, and with crisp Dutch attendants. We took off on the first leg to Vienna, arriving in less than two hours. There we stood at the open doors but were not permitted off the plane. Soon we were in the air again for the much longer flight to Khartoum in the Sudan.

For me Christmas Eve has always been the most magical night of the year. As the plane sped along I thought of the throng assembling at Saint Peter's for midnight mass and of the stores closing at home and families gathering. There was something lacking in the undemonstrative rows of travelers on the plane. Prompted by the seasonal spirit, Tom, Stu and I stood up in the aisle, with reluctant support from the rest of our group, and tried to get our section of the plane started on Christmas carols. It was a futile effort. Except for a few Germans who made a feeble attempt at "O Tannenbaum," we were unable to penetrate the nearly uniform reserve of what suddenly seemed a strange assembly. So we retreated to our seats.

At 3:30 in the morning we reached Khartoum, a city whose lights spread over a surprising expanse below. A few Africans deplaned but the rest of us had to remain on board. All the doors and the cargo hatch near the kitchen were opened, and we went out on the steps of the landing stairs, breathing the fresh air and looking toward the lights of the city. The plane had stopped far from any of the airport buildings, but trucks soon appeared and a dozen Africans scampered aboard through the doors and galley hatch to take off refuse and bring on supplies. They were jet black, lean and tall, adorned in turbans, with white flowing shirts and pants rolled at the bottom, wearing sandals instead of shoes. We felt an eerie thrill as they worked around us. I regretted not having a day to visit Khartoum and neighboring Omdurman. They stand at the confluence of the White and Blue Nile and have a savage, tumultuous history. Here in 1884 Gordon was massacred by the Mahdi, whose monumental tomb is still standing. Here in 1896 the British, a young Winston Churchill in the front line, avenged Gordon's defeat in the last great battle between native spears and modern rifles. It was too bad to miss these historic battlegrounds. Standing on the ramp, a full moon shone down from directly overhead. The air was cool, reminding us that, although approaching the equator, the elevation was high.

Then the plane headed south for Tanzania. I tried to sleep but felt cramped and uncomfortable. A short man with a moustache, resembling a dumpy Hitler, was sitting in front of me. He repeatedly pushed his seat back until it jammed my legs. I pushed it gently forward several times, asking him to avoid the extremes. But he got up often and each time he sat down he pushed the seat back again. Finally I reached up beside him, pressed the latch of his seat, and shoved it completely forward in a manner that could have left no doubt how I felt. He did not even look around. Ellen later talked with him in the aisle and learned that he was a Harvard graduate and a professor (at a New England college I will have the grace not to name) on his way to a holiday safari.

Soon the red African sun was shining through the clouds on the eastern horizon. One of the stewardesses appeared in a mini-skirted Santa Claus outfit of red and white crepe paper, creating a sensation as she handed out certificates for crossing the equator. The flight attendants then brought breakfast. About 10:00 A.M. we approached Kilimanjaro, all of us pressing against the windows to get a look at the famous mountain we had come so far to climb, but clouds over the summit blocked our view. Coming down the steps from the plane, the air was warm and pleasant. Except for the clouds on the mountain, the sky was clear.

The Kilimanjaro International Airport is a small spot in the African plain. It is twenty miles southwest of the mountain and halfway between the town of Moshi twenty miles east and the town of Arusha to the west. The only main road runs between them; there is no direct route to the mountain.

The terminal is a single-story building, with a large observation roof. A line of Africans on the roof watched us as we disembarked. It was only a few steps from the runway to a walk leading into the terminal. Both sides of the walk were decorated with flowers, giving a welcoming touch. We were relieved to stretch in the warm sunshine after the long confinement of the plane and we all paused, rummaging in our hand packs for passports. Tom G. snapped pictures. We might have been tourists arriving on a Caribbean island.

Our first stop was for review and stamping of the arrival forms we had filled out on the plane. Then ensued

41

a lengthy process of passport examination and currency registration. It took nearly forty-five minutes to finish with these routines. Finally, we collected our baggage, which had been deposited in the center of the terminal, and looked up to discover the smiling face of Mr. Lilla, the general manager of the State Travel Service, who had come from Arusha to greet us.

Mr. Lilla was a thin, well-dressed, refined man, with a gentle smile. He spoke in the soft tones of many Africans and Indians taught English by the English and was quite fluent, having no difficulty understanding us. The first project, he said, was to get the women's tickets to Zanzibar so there would be no delay when they came for their flight two days later.

We were ushered to an office and introduced to one of Mr. Lilla's colleagues. She explained that the tickets had to be paid for now so that they could be picked up at plane time. Because it was Christmas, however, she did not have access to a drawer with official receipt forms, and felt incapable of writing out any other form of receipt. Mr. Lilla vouched for himself, for his colleague, and for the tourist agency, but—perhaps for lack of sleep, we explained—we could not bring ourselves to pay now with no receipt and no tickets. Naturally we had full confidence in them but suppose, just suppose, that two days from now Mr. Lilla's colleague was ill, out to lunch, or out of town, and no one was there to prove payment had been made. After a quarter-hour stalemate, it was agreed that payment would be made when the tickets were picked up.

Returning to the main part of the terminal, we heard Swahili spoken for the first time. I have been told it is an easy language to learn, and it is here worth a moment to explain its place among the world's languages and its general characteristics. Most languages belong to one of the great "language families." The Indo-European family, for example, includes the Romance (or Latin) as well as the Teutonic languages; English belongs to that family.

Hebrew, Aramaic, and Arabic belong to the Semitic family, while Chinese, Burmese, Tibetan, and Siamese are members of the Indo-Chinese family. In central and southern Africa a large number of languages, including Swahili, are associated in a Bantu family.

These languages are spoken in Africa from the equator to the Cape, and, despite differences, the roots of many words are the same. For example, the word for "men" in many of the Bantu languages is *aba-ntu,* and this word, which literally means "human being," is the source of the word *Bantu.* The Bantu-speaking area is twice as large as the United States, covering all of Africa below the Eastern bulge. Most of the people who speak it are even today illiterate, and it is therefore astonishing that such a common form of language prevails over such an area. The differences among the Bantu languages are said to be no greater than the differences between Spanish and Italian. Equally surprising is the fact that the Bantu languages have changed little over the centuries. In 1624, a missionary prepared a catechism in Congolese, one of the Bantu dialects. That document, compared to today's Congolese, shows little change. (So much for the argument that unwritten languages are more subject to change than written ones.) The real impetus to language changes arises from a changing or migrating society exposed to new objects, circumstances, and conditions. This has not been the experience of the people of Africa.

Swahili was originally the dialect of Zanzibar, the word *Swahile* coming from the Arabic word *sawahel,* which means "coasts." It worked its way inland with Arab traders, who for centuries have frequented the African coast and, until early in this century, raided the interior for slaves. Thirty million people now speak Swahili, which includes many Arabic words, as well as the Arab alphabet, in which respect it is similar to English.

Swahili differs from most languages by lacking both articles and gender. Instead, the nouns are grouped into some twenty "classes," each class having its own prefix. For example, one noun class begins with *m* in the singular and *wa* in the plural. This class generally denotes human beings. The word for man or person is *mtu,* for wife *mke,* for child *mtoto.* The plurals are *watu, wake* and *watoto.* Linguists think the prefixes may have once been independent words with a specific meaning, standing for a number of objects belonging to a single group, such as human beings. Constant use may have caused contraction through the dropping of intermediate letters, leaving only the first letter of the original definite article. Hence, the *m* of the class described. The letter prefixes, however, now perform a grammatical function by changing the singular to the plural and making various other changes in a sentence. Where English makes the change at the end of the word, Swahili makes the change at the beginning. Adjectives agree with their nouns both in number and in their nominal prefixes. This type of word classification is characteristic of languages which have not been required to develop refinements in a more flexible pattern.

All Swahili words seem to end in vowels, and in most cases this produces a pleasant and satisfying sound—a completeness in pronunciation—as in Italian. The basic words and expressions are easy to learn and we picked up a few even on our short visit. One quickly says *asante,* or "thank you," and even sooner, *jambo,* which means "hello," or "good morning." The most important climbing word is *poli, poli,* or "slowly."

Emerging from the terminal for our first close-up view of Africa, we saw before us that universal vista—a large asphalt parking lot! It was filled with vehicles, drivers leaning against them, smoking and chatting in the sun. On this familiar footing, the twelve of us, strung out with fourteen pieces of luggage and assortments of handpacks, approached our two Volkswagen vans. Mr. Lilla introduced our two drivers, Frank and Stephen. Frank was about forty, with a moonlike face, open smile, and pleasant manner. He had the *joie de vivre* that brightens life for himself and all around him. Stephen, about the same age, had a strong face and was more reserved. Both spoke some English, but neither was as fluent as Mr. Lilla. Before leaving, we reviewed our itinerary with the drivers and Mr. Lilla, using the sheets we had been given in New York. Everything seemed to be understood and in order.

Driving out to the main road and turning east toward Moshi, one's first impression is of the enormous dimension of Africa. The dry brown plains spread off to the horizon and, except for the cloud cover on Kilimanjaro, nothing dilutes the feeling of endless expanse. We could have been on the plains of the moon. Shortly, we saw walking by the road decorated natives, as if they had stepped out of the nineteenth century. "Masai, this their territory," Frank explained. They were tall and thin, dressed in red togas, with glistening black skin and hair that must have been dipped in grease.

The Masai are the most famous and interesting of the East African tribes. Their origin is obscure but some have traced it to the intermarriage of a tall, light-skinned race known as the Hamite with the Nilotes, a Negro people of the Nile River Basin. Hundreds, perhaps thousands, of years ago they migrated south, defeating those in their path. Like many races before and since, they invested avarice with the trappings of doctrine and adopted the creed that all cattle should be theirs. Cattle raiding became the national game. Today the Masai occupy a large area of Tanzania from Kilimanjaro west to the Serengeti Plain. Their territory also extends north into Kenya. The portion below Kilimanjaro appears on maps as the Masai Steppe.

It is startling, even in Africa, to drive out of an airport and immediately see a Masai herdsman with a spear or stick, tending his cattle. They give the impression of being backward people with no facility for becoming civilized. But this is exactly the opposite of the reason for their distinctive character. Far from being incapable bush natives, the Masai regard themselves, like the Jews, as the chosen people, and believe in the coming of a Messiah. They are proud and tough, and it is due to their religious traditions and clannishness that they have resisted the modern world. Those watching us drive by did not look envious.

In the nineteenth century, explorers and missionaries had a difficult time with the Masai, who demanded tribute for crossing their territory. The missionaries, despite long efforts, gained few converts. The Arab traders passed through the Masai lands and westward into the far interior, having learned long before that the Masai could not be enslaved. Today there are about 200,000 Masai and while there are undoubtedly many young deserters from their ranks, to a large extent they continue to live in their own way, resistant to modern notions of progress.

The Masai depend on cattle for everything. In periods of drought and when food is scarce, they drink cow blood to obtain protein and iron. The cattle recover quickly from the blood drawing procedure, which is carried out by a strap around the neck and an arrow pushed into the jugular vein. One crudely useful practice of the Masai is to pull two teeth from the bottom of each person's mouth so that if lockjaw occurs, milk or blood can be poured in.

The Masai are famous for putting red clay on their legs and a coppery tinge of red ocher in their hair. They also spread animal fat on their body and that, with the ocher, acts as insulation against both heat and cold and gives their skin a silken quality.

In herding their cattle, the average Masai tribesman walks twenty-six miles a day—the distance of a marathon. They are probably the world's premier example of a people in A-plus cardiovascular condition. Dr. George Mann of Vanderbilt University, an expert in heart disease and exercise, tested Masai tribesmen and found that the average man could keep up with a treadmill 60 percent longer than his American college counterpart.

Frank and Stephen were both members of the Chagga tribe, which occupies the eastern, southern, and part of the western slopes of Kilimanjaro. The Chaggas are civilized, organized, and businesslike. They are prolific coffee growers and good merchants. Their schools are well attended and their tribal organization, solid and sophisticated. They have their own flag, national anthem, and federated organizations. Most are Christians and Frank told me he was a Catholic. All the Africans we saw near Kilimanjaro, apart from the Masai, were Chaggas.

The Chaggas and Masai occupy adjacent and indeed, overlapping territories. The differences between them illustrate how principles more than environment shape the lives of individuals and groups.

Soon clusters of houses began to appear and we saw a number of "regular" Africans walking on the side of the road. We were approaching Moshi, a town of about 10,000. As we neared the more inhabited area, we came to a traffic circle, the center decorated with flowers. On the outside perimeter, trees and bushes shaded what looked like comfortable, single-story houses. The town seems to have been well planned and some of the buildings well built, but in the sluggish equatorial climate, and in the decades since the British left, the grass has grown more freely, repairs have been made less often, and the streets and buildings have acquired a worn look. Still, the town was alive with people, walking at a leisurely gait.

Then we arrived at the Moshi Hotel. In British times, it was called the Livingstone, and the name still appears in big letters at the top of the building. We walked up the veranda steps into a small airy lobby. A wispy African pine tree, decorated with paper ornaments and puffs of cotton, was lighted for Christmas. But the surroundings were so alien that only with a conscious effort could I recall it was Christmas Day. At the reception desk, an attendant produced the reservation book and we signed in. Then we were directed upstairs, assured that our luggage would follow. We reached the three upper floors by means of a circular stairway of painted cement steps, many of which had clots of mud tracked in from the outside. The upper hallways were bright and spacious, with windows at either end; the rooms were large, but sparsely furnished and without charm. Screenless windows offered a view over the rooftops of the town. Not far away I saw a minaret.

Frank had told me there was a Catholic church just up a gravel road from the hotel. It was now noon and, despite our travels, I hoped to attend a Christmas mass. So I left immediately to scout for the church. Well-dressed Africans, including many children, were coming toward me. None of them stared or took special notice although a white man could not have been a common sight. At the end of the gravel road I saw the church, a long cinderblock building with a carefully carved frame entrance. I went in the front door but was stopped immediately by a beautiful wooden gate that reached from floor to ceiling and blocked off the interior. The church was empty except for two white-robed women near the sanctuary, who seemed to be cleaning up. Going around the side, I met two well-dressed men and asked if there was another Mass. They said the last one had just ended. Not certain they had understood me, I continued to the back entrance where one of the white-gowned women confirmed the report.

When I returned, the others were ready for lunch and we went into the large uncrowded dining room. There were two or three black couples and a small group of Japanese. We had a warm drink that was like Coca-Cola, cow soup, some tough bread, and beef for the main course. Dessert was mangoes, a pearlike fruit plentiful in Tanzania. Afterwards, we slept through the afternoon.

When we came down for dinner at 7:00, the lobby was crowded. A man at a table on the left was behind a sign announcing that "Dinner-Dance" tickets were available. Another sign at the dining-room door stated that "Dinner-Dance" tickets were required. On the opposite side of the lobby was a large dark room with a bar at one end and glass doors opening to a patio; this was the site of the Christmas dance. It required much effort to explain that we were eating dinner rather than going to the dance, the table man politely stating over and over that the only tickets he had were "Dinner-Dance" tickets. Eventually, another attendant appeared at the dining room and, more comprehending, admitted us without tickets. There we had an interesting and tasty dinner of questionable origin. A problem in Africa, as in many foreign countries, is that one develops a craving for salad and other uncooked items that cannot safely be eaten. Thirst also becomes an obsession and has to be quenched with one of the local colas, which are

49

usually served lukewarm. Not being a beer drinker, I could not appreciate the local banana beer, which did well for some of the others. After dinner, Linda and the younger men were invited to the dance. They were the only white people, but they were courteously treated and made to feel at home. The music included some American songs, but most was a combination of African and European melodies. Although everyone seemed well behaved, we noticed that there were soldiers with rifles in the lobby and outside the front door. The crowd was in good spirits and none of us felt any sense of unease. But we were too tired to stay long. Nor did the music or noise reach our rooms.

About 5:00 A.M. while it was still dark, I was awakened by a distant wailing cry. Peering out the window, it eventually registered that the cry came from the minaret and was the first prayer of the new day. It lasted only a few minutes, and I went back to sleep.

A buffet breakfast of mangoes, orange juice, and toast was set up in the dining room. We also had scrambled eggs, which were almost pure white. Waiting in the lobby for Frank and Stephen who appeared at nine o'clock, Roland counted over one hundred empty beer bottles on the tables in the dance room. Men were cleaning the floor by flooding it with a hose. In the lobby, broken glass had been swept up, but beer dropped the night before was still splotched on the floor.

Chapter 7
The Kibo Hotel

Heading out from Moshi we were soon in flat, dry country. The roadside that passed before us was a variegated scene of huts of mud and straw, modern houses, children, adults, and goats, all appearing in random sequence along the route. At a few stores people waited for buses but the main impression was that everyone walked. This pedestrian society had none of the impersonal bustle of the city. It seemed pervasively social.

As we drove east, Kilimanjaro to the north remained wrapped in clouds. After fifteen miles we reached the hamlet of Himo and turned north toward Marangu, in the foothills southeast of the mountain. The shoulder of Kilimanjaro slopes eastward from the summit and the trail we were to take follows the shoulder, but both summit and shoulder remained in the mist. Frank said the rains were late this year, and that for weeks he had not been able to see the mountain.

All around us, however, the sun was shining. As we moved upward from 3,000 to 5,000 feet, and onto an elevation with more rain, the vegetation thickened. Banana trees appeared, each with thick, distinctively short bananas. Underneath, smaller coffee trees grew, their red beans shining in the sun. Cows, goats, and chickens looked out at us from the yards of huts and houses. This hill area was more thickly settled and people were on both sides of the road. The women wore multi-colored skirts and dresses; many carried bunches of bananas or baskets on their heads. The men, too, were often in suits and ties, and large congregations of children, the girls in white dresses, appeared everywhere. Frank said the day after Christmas was a holiday, and the people were coming from church and other festivities. It was curious to see a primitive hut on one lot and a substantial house on the next, a tattered dress on one woman and a colorful ensemble on another. As this kaleidoscope of humanity passed by, I was struck with the poise and posture of those we passed. Everyone seemed part of an active and happy community and was busy at work or play. Extremely poor materially, they were not poor in spirit. Groups of younger men waved and shouted at our vans, the local sport being to call for a ride on any passing vehicle. Frank proudly said, "Chagga people."

The Kibo Hotel is a graceful white two-story building set against a hill and facing south toward a green valley and the plains. A large garden extends across the front, and at one side there is a low-walled walkway to the entrance. Pictures of the mountain and some early German climbers are on the walls of the inside hall. The dining room looks out over the garden. On the opposite side of the hall is a spacious lounge. Upstairs, the rooms are open and comfortable, each with its own balcony. Animal skin covers are on the beds. An airy rustic African charm pervades the premises. For us the hotel had the added excitement of being the outfitting base from which we would set off on our climb. Natives were strolling in the road in front and lounging in the garden and on the walls of the walkway.

We were soon on our balconies taking pictures, and admiring the flowers and view. After getting settled, several of us went up the road, nodding to the people and examining the banana and coffee trees. Everything was civilized but with a strange and unfamiliar cast. Many of the natives spoke broken English; all appeared courteous, dignified, and at ease. This was, after all, their country, their village, and their home.

We came upon a large group, including young girls and boys dressed in white, standing on either side of the road in front of a church. The service had just concluded and they were lined up in a formal departure ceremony. We held back to watch. Farther along we saw an open stone building that might have been a church but turned out to be a courtroom. There were no benches inside but it had an elevated stage with a tree stump that was the "dock." In the rear was a small cell. A boy who lived across the road greeted us and explained in good English that the magistrate came from time to time to hold local court.

On our way back we stopped at an open shed with a tin roof. It held a rusted tank from which extended a sheetmetal spout. This was equipment for making banana beer or, as it is called, "safari beer."

Some of our group got ahead of us, and when we reached the top of a hill, they were out of sight. They continued on past the hotel, looking for a waterfall reportedly nearby. After wandering about, they met a man who volunteered to be a guide and told them the waterfall was only a short distance away, down one of the trails. So they followed him over streams and up and down hills, past huts and families who smiled greetings. "Not much more, not much more," he kept saying. After forty minutes, they reached a spectacular waterfall. When they got back, he bargained for a fee and they ended up paying him $10—a sum that probably tripled his monthly earnings.

Meanwhile, Roland had stayed at the hotel with his father and Tom Jr. His diary caught the scene:

Tommy had brought with him a *Sports Illustrated* with an article on the attempt to climb Everest without oxygen. I hung around when the others went on a walk and read that. Then John, who had not gone on the walk, read it also.

Finally, Tommy, who had returned from a walk, and Dad ended up getting into one of those deep conversations. Tommy had explained his whole situation with————. (He even pulled out his "Please be happy for me letter" from————after she had gotten married.) So after that they analyzed women and their actions and reactions. Then I left because of boredom. . . . *

After lunch, Stu met an Englishman who had just returned from the summit. He was in his thirties, strong and mature in manner, and was writing letters in the lounge. On the walls were spears, shields, and animal heads. Stu rounded me up and together we pumped him for information. He said the snow and rain had added to the challenge of the climb, that there was wood for a fire at the first hut, a little at the second, and none at the third. We could expect to be wet and should take all possible care to keep dry and warm. He mentioned the mud on the first few days of the trail, and the need for waterproofing on our boots. He urged us to wear gaiters to keep out the mud, and later the snow. We were far into the conversation before we learned that his group had spent two extra days high up before attempting the summit. Even so, two of the women with him had not made the top. It was cold at the top—although he did not know the temperature—and ice on the crater rim had prevented him from reaching Uruhu. He said it would be good to have candles; I did not appreciate his remark, to my later regret. He and his four companions were not staying at the hotel, but lived in a van parked nearby. They had left England in June, had driven across Europe to North Africa, and then through Africa to Kilimanjaro. He said they

*Reprinted by permission of Roland M. Hartzell.

had "lost" two members along the way: one in Algeria where, learning of a family illness, the man had returned home; the other in Uganda, where, while changing a tire, the man had been killed by another vehicle. These "losses brought us closer together," he added oddly. "So far," he calculated, "the last six months have cost me the equivalent of only $1,500 U.S."

In the hall, we met an American teenager and his mother. The father worked in Kenya, and over the holidays mother and son had come down with friends to climb. Two days of rain on the trail and they had turned back; they were now heading home to Nairobi. They gave a gloomy report of the trail and difficulties.

We asked at the reception desk about gaiters and rain equipment. The attendant said everything would be discussed at a 5:00 P.M. "briefing." This had the right ring. So we idled away the afternoon reading, resting, and getting organized. From our balcony, Mary Lee painted the southern view.

At five o'clock sharp, we crowded into the manager's office behind the reception desk—all except Stu, who had not heard the time and was taking a nap. A middle-aged Canadian couple and their companion, a thin man in his thirties with a constant smile, were already there. The manager, Godfrey Labrosse, an intelligent and cultured man who spoke excellent English, explained that at this season—meaning the week between Christmas and New Year's—a flood of hikers were trying to climb the mountain. Park rangers reported the huts were filled and people were being turned away to fend for themselves in the wet and cold. The local youths were partying and it was difficult to get porters. None of this made any difference to us. We had come 11,000 miles, had a schedule that could not be changed, and unless the Almighty moved the mountain itself out of our reach, we intended to climb it. It was merely a matter of how to deal with the problems, not whether we would go up. The Canadian woman, glum looking for a mountain climber, remarked plaintively, "Why don't the travel authorities tell people this is a bad week to climb." Godfrey agreed they should have, and assured us he would do his best to complete arrangements for guides and porters. He then ran through the list of clothes and equipment we would need. Next he took us to his storeroom, where he picked out extra blankets for those with lighter sleeping bags, rubberized pants and gaiters, day packs for Tom and his sons, and other miscellaneous equipment. The storeroom was inadequate for complete outfitting but we had brought virtually everything we needed. As we left the room, Godfrey handed each of us a wooden hiking stick with a steel tip. This had a sporting touch. I took mine in jaunty ignorance of the vital role it would later play.

Seated at a table for twelve we had an excellent dinner, all agreeing it had been a stimulating day. Tom Jr. took pictures of the smiling group—the women ready for Zanzibar, the men eager for the climb. Nearby were three young Japanese, two men and a woman. Stu, his antennae ever ready, heard they had come down that day, not having made the summit. I stopped at their table and asked how the climb had gone. They said they had gotten beyond the third hut but the snow and cold had forced them to turn back. Nothing they said hinted of danger. They looked fine and were in good spirits.

After dinner, on another reconnaissance, Stu found two Swedish couples in their twenties, all four of whom had reached the top. We surrounded them seeking details, especially about how they felt at various altitudes. They admitted nausea, vomiting and headaches, but assured us it "was not so bad." Then it came out they had spent three extra days on the way up. This convinced us that five days was too short. We located Godfrey and told him that we needed an extra day at the second hut. This meant returning a day later and meeting the women Sunday night at the Ngorongoro Wildlife Lodge, instead of for Sunday lunch at Arusha. Godfrey agreed and said he would make arrangements with the guides and porters. Frank was out front with his friends and we explained our change of plans. The schedule was now locked in place.

Chapter 8
Forward and Up

Mary Lee was awake through the night with stomach problems. She took pills prescribed in Scarsdale, but they had no immediate effect and she did not go down for breakfast. I joined the others in the dining room.

The men were taut with the start close upon us. "Can you believe we're actually here and going to do this!" Stu asked. "I can't," said Tom G. Tom alone looked relaxed. I do not recall ever seeing him otherwise; in circumstances placid or turbulent, hearing news good or bad, facing pleasant or disagreeable tasks, his cheerful approach seems to balance the occasion. Alice is much the same, and I have wondered since whether those friends who see them in their normal social habitat realize, as our adventures were to prove, their underlying strengths.

I brought tea and toast to Mary Lee. She was in a humorously miserable state worrying about the two-hour ride in the van and then the flight, with a change of planes in Dar es Salaam, to Zanzibar. When the others were ready, and with Frank waiting sympathetically at the van, she came down and curled up in the back seat. We assured her the worst must be over, and that Zanzibar would be paradise. I was a little uneasy, but knew the others would take care of her and that she would survive any embarrassments.

After the women left, we went back to Godfrey's office. I looked down the cloister-like porchway that extends along the back of the hotel and the rear gardens. Large sacks of food, interspersed with pieces of equipment, were stacked in a long line. Some of the sacks had been further

59

stuffed into heavy red plastic bags, and these in turn had been put into coarse gunny sacks. This colorful, multi-layer wrapping of supplies on a warm sunny day foretold a less hospitable climate above. In a pantry near the rear kitchen, Godfrey was packing boxes of food, which porters carried out and added to the supply line. The sacks were large and bulky. They had neither straps nor handles, and there were an amazing number. Our group would include eight hikers, twelve porters and three guides. There were two smaller groups—the three Canadians, and a group of four Frenchmen—for whom Godfrey was also making preparations. With guides and porters this meant about forty people altogether, with food, clothing, and equipment, including pots, lanterns, and other accessories, for five or six days. The scale of the preparations spiced the atmosphere.

The porters stood around, seemingly unconcerned at the daunting task which lay before them. I felt the relief that comes with knowing that a problem is not mine. A great feature of this climb: if I got myself, camera, canteen, and poncho up the mountain, nothing else was expected. Daily life often demands more. In my prior experiences, I had been my own porter and cook, and had suffered the consequences of incompetence and exhaustion at high altitudes where, among other annoyances, one can die of starvation or boredom waiting for water to boil.

After he finished with the food, Godfrey organized the troops. One of the Frenchmen, an outgoing, strongly built man in his late thirties, told me his group of four had been assigned to ours if we were agreeable. We said that would be fine, hoping for a chance to practice French and with little other thought to what was involved. But in a few minutes he returned to say that Godfrey had altered the plan and they would go separately. It is hard to say what the outcome might have been if they had been with us higher up. The Canadians must also have been given separate guides and porters, because I did not see them again until the end of the first day at the Mandara Huts. Our packs, which had been placed in the entrance hall, were now moved out with the food and equipment to the gravel area in front. Ten or twelve young porters were standing around the baggage. A man from the hotel came out, looking for the "leader" of our group. He asked me to go to Godfrey's office to meet our guides. All of us went in and Godfrey introduced Effatta, our chief guide, and Fred and Felix, his assistants. Effatta was small and partly bald; he smiled broadly as we shook hands and seemed anxious to please. Fred and Felix were younger and more reserved. All wore nondescript clothes and only their ages distinguished them from the porters. Without knowledge of the guides' duties, I assumed they signed us in at the "Gate" of Kilimanjaro National Park and showed us the way up the mountain, where no one was likely to get lost anyhow. My expectation, based principally on Tarzan movies, was that we were in charge and that the guides and porters did the work. Pointing to Effatta, Godfrey said, "He's small but he's the best." Effatta beamed.

Out front, I met my porter, a medium-size sixteen-year-old named Livingstone. He did not try to speak English, although he understood me and quickly took my pack, plus a lantern and other items that someone had added. Livingstone and the others, many of whom were barefoot, wore an assortment of cast-off clothes. But their alert expressions and fluid movements hinted at splendidly conditioned bodies. None appeared robust or overly muscular, but we were soon to see how easily they carried their enormous loads. We later saw barefoot porters with both packs on their backs and sacks on their heads move up the muddy trail.

The Gate was a half-hour's walk from the hotel. Tom G. had struck up an acquaintance with one of the women with the Englishman we had met in the lounge. She had finished breakfast at the hotel and came out to offer us a ride in a small pickup. Our porters wanted to climb in too, with the packs and food, but the truck could not accommodate us all. Rather than risk resentment by riding off without them, we declined her invitation. The woman, however, took our picture, and looking at it now I can see again the enthusiasm which animated us all. Our simple hiking sticks are held casually, with Tom's raised in cheery salute. Then Stephen drove up in his van and said he would shuttle all of us to the Gate.

The Gate is no more than a sign hanging from a log elevated above the road, like the entrance to a western ranch. Low buildings on either side of the road serve as park headquarters. One structure has an open side; everyone must register there before starting to climb. More than a hundred climbers were milling around, either preparing to start or returning from above. There was an even greater number of guides, porters and other Africans. Swahili, French, German, Japanese, English and other languages could be heard. It might have been the construction site for the Tower of Babel. A large contingent of hikers, whom I took to be French and whom we later learned worked in Central Africa, were climbing down from a truck. Expecting to see them from time to time on the way up, I suggested to one woman that if she spoke in English I would respond in French. She agreed, but I soon realized that she needed no practice in speaking English. Her two sons looked at me condescendingly.

This group got off quickly, as did several others, including the Canadians and the four Frenchmen. We were delayed waiting for Stephen to bring our porters and guides. Each of us signed the register; then we filled canteens at a nearby stream, dropping in purification tablets despite assurances that the water was clean. Tom spilled tablets in the heavy grass but we retrieved most of them. Some Americans had just come down, their legs and boots caked with mud. We compared starting in low shoes and saving our boots for higher up with the alternatives, matters having gotten down to ultimate practicalities. Eventually, our guides and porters arrived. Effatta, whose name I had forgotten, cleared matters at the registration office.

The trail entrance, like the park entrance one hundred yards before, is marked by a horizontal log above the roadway. There were buffalo heads attached to each of the vertical supports. The trail was wide and smooth, the upward grade moderate. We were in a forest of thick trees and vines, with flowers and singing birds. Our porters, balancing sacks on their heads, reached up now and then to steady their loads. They glided along even on steep sections, and would have qualified as instructors at charm schools where aspiring actresses are taught to walk gracefully. As our own and other porters moved casually and effortlessly by us, it was clear that they were in their milieu. Some had tee shirts with Michigan State, UCLA, and other familiar names. I could not tell, and never discovered later, where they carried warmer clothes for the higher altitudes, and none of them had sleeping bags or blankets or indeed anything for the cold nights. I could not distinguish our guides from the others; someone reminded me of Effatta's name, which I had not seen written and kept forgetting. Later I was told he was behind us, but I did not realize for two days that he stayed last to be sure we were all safe.

The Gate is at 5,900 feet and, not feeling the altitude, there was a great temptation to move along at a normal pace. But I realized that my chance of reaching the top depended on holding to a stiflingly slow pace from the start, never moving fast enough to require even a moderately deep breath or any noticeable muscular exertion. This itself demands a repressive effort when one feels gung ho and others pass by, walking normally. Most in our group were holding back, too, but none was as slow as I, and so I fell behind. Once I looked back and saw Effatta. He was walking in a crouch, leaning on his cane, his steps slow.

In an hour I caught up to Peter and Roland, who had stopped because Roland was developing heel blisters. I had some moleskin, which Peter cut to size. Later, I reached those in the lead, including some of the porters, who had stopped for lunch. Godfrey had given us small packets with crustless egg sandwiches, a hard-boiled egg, a banana, and mangoes. Nearby, a good-looking Swedish woman and her teenage sons were having lunch by a stream that bubbled down the hill. Although the trail was now narrow and the rain forest dense, spread down the line with colorful packs and bags we might have been on a picnic anywhere.

The grade became steeper as the trail turned into the stream bed. The rocks got larger and the mud thicker. We moved up the side of a hill, down across a ravine, up another stream bed. The trees, despite their density, were more like a forest than a jungle except for the profusion of vines. Someone saw a monkey but I saw only an occasional bird.

It began to rain, lightly at first but soon in a steady pour, with occasional stinging hail. Yellow, orange, and blue ponchos appeared ahead. Tom Jr.'s and Roland's ponchos were strapped around their sleeping bags and the rain and hail beat down on their tee shirts and shorts. The trail became a carpet of mud. My poncho was light but covered my day pack and movie camera, which was in a separate case. Using my stick like an awning brace, I held the bottom of the poncho over my feet. It was a losing effort, and the steady downpour soaked my legs and boots. Soon I stopped looking around and concentrated on moving slowly, resisting the urge to hurry. I slipped several times, catching myself but only by means of the spurts of energy I was trying to avoid using. About four o'clock, we passed through an area of wet bushes and trees, and after a steep rise over still another hill, reached the Mandara Huts.

The huts were on a grassy level where the slope pauses before resuming its persistent rise. The main hut was a large, one-room A-frame with tables and benches along either side of the interior and a Franklin-type stove near the rear. Behind it was a ladder stairway to a loft that had a central walkway with double decker slab bunks on either side, twenty-eight in all. Outside were smaller, four-bunk A-frames, and beyond them on one side were huts for cooking and for the guides and porters.

The main hut was crowded with people shedding their wet clothes. Learning that the caretaker was nearby, I went to inquire where we could bunk. Shrugging, he told me in broken English there were sixty-three bunks but that over ninety hikers had already arrived. With the rain coming down, I was too wet and cold to squander my remaining energy in protest or frustration. In the meantime, Tom Jr. and Roland had looked, without success, for bunks in the smaller huts. When I heard there were none we decided to sleep on the floor of the main A-frame and went to stake out our spots. As we headed over I saw Effatta. He was holding some papers which I took to be our "reservations," and was soon protesting to the caretaker the lack of space for his group. Effatta was now entirely different from the grinning little man we had met at the hotel. His authoritative bearing, and the attention he received from the caretaker and the porters, showed that he was an important figure on the mountain. Still, the caretaker could not evict those who had bunks and who had as much right to them as we did. Nor could anyone justly criticize the officials at the Gate. Godfrey had told us the huts were overcrowded and people did not have bunks. For all I knew the Gate officials had repeated this to Effatta and to the guides for other groups. In fact, we had been scheduled to start early in order to reach the huts ahead of other hikers but our delay had allowed the large French-speaking group and undoubtedly many others to get ahead. Most of these hikers, like us, had come a long way to climb the mountain and none was deterred by warnings of overcrowding. Any minor disappointment was quickly submerged in the pleasant realization that we were not weighted down with the usual concern for a hot shower and a warm bed. Freed of such appendages and most other routines of civilized living—traveling light, in that respect—contributed to the carefree attitude that was a main attraction of the climb. Floor space in one hut was as good as a slab in another. I told Effatta we would sleep in the main hut.

The rain had diminished, starting up occasionally as grey clouds gusted by at eye level. Now and then the sun blinked through. The temperature was in the fifties and it was not unpleasant. Although my boots and poncho were soaked and muddy and underneath I was awash in sweat, I felt invigorated. Livingstone, whom I had not seen since the start, had left my pack in the main hut so I peeled down and put on dry clothes. The bottom of my pack was wet and water had penetrated part of my sleeping bag but the clothes in the middle had been wrapped separately in plastic and were dry. On a nearby table, Tom, still in wet clothes, was carefully separating sheets of airplane tickets, passports, and money, and squeezing out the water.

Hikers were still coming up the trail and pushing into

the main hut. It might have been a Swiss ski lodge at lunchtime except for the Africans in rubber and plastic ponchos, many with goggles, who were pouring in and dumping the packs. Some beautiful bodies were briefly on display as wet clothes were changed, but people were too busy for modesty or embarrassment. The multi-lingual chatter enlivened the scene. Several hikers were working at a fire in the small stove, but they could make little of it with only damp sticks and brush available. Felix and some of our other porters took our boots and sleeping bags to the cooking huts, where the fires were larger. They were warm but still wet when returned. In the late afternoon the rain stopped and ponchos and jackets were hung on the deck railings. Moisture from low clouds, however, countered the drying breeze.

All in all, it was a lively international assemblage both in and outside the hut. Everyone soon looked warm and dry. Most even looked stylish, in sharp contrast to their matted hair and bedraggled appearance on arrival.

Our group spread out at the back of the hut. On the left, at a table near the back window, a Swiss family was munching snacks. The mother and her adult daughter looked the same age, and the father appeared not much older than the daughter's boyfriend. The parents were from Dar es Salaam, and the daughter and her boyfriend were visiting from Zurich for the holidays. They had beaten the crowd up the trail, had gotten bunks, and now, neatly dressed, were, as John put it, "just hanging." They said they would be moving out later and we could use their table as a bed.

Felix then appeared, surprising us with a print table-cloth which he spread on the table next to the Swiss family; from a gunny sack, he drew plastic cups and saucers. A minute later he returned with a pot of tea and coarse, tasty cookies. This turn of events after an altogether primitive day gave new meaning to an old ritual:

> Under certain circumstances there are few hours in life more agreeable than the hour dedicated to the ceremony known as afternoon tea. There are circumstances in which, whether you partake of the tea or not—some people of course never do—the situation is in itself delightful.*

We, of course, partook extensively, having sweated quarts in the day's effort. Replenished, we went out front to watch the hikers who were still emerging from the forest below. With the improving weather I also walked down toward the trail, and was able to take movies of the hut and those on the deck as the setting sun appeared in the west. Later on I learned how much of the social whirl had passed me by. During tea, the daughter of the Swiss couple, with her boyfriend sitting on her left, quickly got acquainted with Tom Jr. and Tom G. on her right. At the same time, John noticed one of the girls with the large French-speaking group, who had managed to capture all the bunks in the loft. He moved across the room and introduced himself, only to find that the girl spoke no English. She was the daughter of the Belgian ambassador to Bwanda, and was hiking with her brother and mother, who was Russian. She spoke French, Russian, and Flemish. John, appreciating possibly for the first time the value of a liberal arts education, quickly shifted into French. The two of them chatted together and then walked out on the deck. Unaware of all this, I caught them with my movie camera when they emerged from the hut.

*The Portrait of a Lady, by Henry James.

Watching the crowd we saw three groups, who, having found no bunks, were preparing to start back down the mountain. There were no more than thirty minutes of daylight left. Nor did I see any guides or porters with them. They disappeared down the trail, and I heard no later reports of difficulty.

Soon Felix reappeared with dinner. We first had soup. Only those who have spent a day hiking in the rain can fully appreciate the rejuvenating impact of the hot, thick liquid going down one's gullet. Beef, liver, carrots, potatoes, bread, and tea followed, with a mango fruit cup for desert. The quantities were ample. Except for a few passing waves of nausea, we enjoyed the dinner. Our systems were idling smoothly; now refueled, we felt ready to start again, and the night seemed like an unwelcome interlude.

And so it turned out. By 6:30 it was dark inside the hut, and we lacked the candles mentioned by the Englishman. The Swedish family had long since departed and Tom, his sons, and Tom G. had put their bags in the back corner. Most other hikers had also eaten and left. I had spread my sleeping bag on a table, Peter's was on a nearby bench barely the width of his body, and John had placed his on a table across the room. Stu was on the floor behind the loft stairway, having moved once because two people had slipped on the muddy steps. I was over talking to Tom when I noticed my sleeping bag had been moved and my table was being pulled away. A cloddish teenager from the French-speaking group had tossed my sleeping bag on a bench and was moving the table. When I protested, he insisted, "We must eat." I heatedly assured him, "I must sleep," and he couldn't take my bed. In the meantime, other members of his group were coming into the hut and filling the benches along the opposite side of the room. The noise grew. At that time I had no idea of their number, or that they were the hikers we had seen at the Gate.

The teenager relinquished my table, but several of the adults asked John for his table so they could push four together on the far side. He agreed on their commitment to return it at the end of an hour—a promise they promptly forgot. John then moved to a narrow bench near me, and we tried to settle down for the night. But the diners chattering in French made sleep impossible. I dozed fitfully and at one point looked over, relieved to see that they appeared finished. As their loud talk persisted, I finally called over and asked them in polite, if awkward, French to go to bed. John also yelled "fatigué." This produced hoots and laughter; only then did I despairingly realize that their dinner had not even started. Another half-hour and their porters finally brought in cauldrons of stew, one porter carrying a lantern and two porters holding each cauldron. Nearly another two hours passed before they finally finished and ambled off to their bunks, their disregard for us leaving behind a solid deposit of ill will. At the time we thought they were French, and Stu said at breakfast the following morning that the next time Germany invades France, we should let them keep it.

Lying on the hard table in the dark, the hut finally quiet, I was ashamed to think that these people could so annoy me. But there is an undeniable satisfaction in feasting on such resentments by contemplating such criticisms as one can muster. I felt suddenly critical of the French generally, and of the haughty manner they often show toward Americans, especially in Paris. This may be the injured pride from two wars, for there is no surer route to resentment than putting someone in your debt if they cannot repay.

I remember, however, an entirely different attitude in

Normandy. When we were there a few years before, the people were warm and still consciously grateful, four decades after D-Day. Although eye witnesses were dying off, there remained a strong awareness of the sacrifices that were made for the liberation of France. The American graveyard at Saint Lo and the museums near the invasion beaches keep history fresh. At Saint Mere Eglise, the entrance to the small airborne museum is the door into a glider that carried some of the first Americans into France. Tacked to the inside wall is a mimeographed sheet, now in a plastic cover but otherwise as it was on the night of June 5, 1944, with the names of those who came in that glider and the seating position each was assigned. A few miles east on the Cherbourg peninsula, the road leading to the sea has posts, each of which bears the name of an American soldier killed on the advance inland. At the end of the road is a large parking area bordering on what was Utah Beach. An inconspicuous quonset hut is another museum, filled with pictures and artifacts of the invasion. Not far away, where the beach begins, there is a stubby robot-shaped cement post. It is painted a grey-pink. It stands alone before the empty stretch of sand and sea. On this insignificant monument are inscribed the sparse but thunderous words:

Ici en debarqué
les Armées American
6 Juin 1944

Sleepless on the hard table, I thought those loud Frenchmen might improve their manners if they visited the invasion beaches.

Chapter 9
The Horombo Huts

Before dawn Effatta sent Fred and one of the porters off for the Horombo Huts to reserve our bunks for the next night. By 6:00, in semi-darkness, we were organizing our gear. This time I emptied my pack and wrapped each item separately in plastic. It was troublesome because of the poor light and the care required not to drop things on the wet floor. The table was crowded with others doing the same.

We had our daily conference over whether to wear boots or low shoes. My boots were still wet but nonetheless felt warm and comfortable once on. I could not see hiking up the rocky trails in running shoes because a sprained ankle could end the climb.

With daylight came Felix and his tablecloth, which he spread over my "bunk," setting out fruit, bread, and marmalade. Moments later he brought porridge, hard-boiled eggs, and tea. The hot food quickly swept away the listlessness from a bad night's sleep. Outside it was wet, inside it was crowded; we were still disorganized, with our packs only partly together; but, instead of having to fix breakfast, here it was before us as in an officers' mess.

Each of us agreed he had not slept and had lain awake all night, enduring till morning. And so it had seemed. Tom was the usual exception. On their narrow benches, Peter or John would have been on the floor with a single false move. Others had similar problems. Nevertheless, we were in top spirits and a breakfast photo taken by Tom G. caught our ebullience.

Where the rest of the climber overflow slept I never discovered. In the light I saw for the first time that the only others who had slept in the hut were an American man and his two teenage daughters. The girls looked fresh. We saw more of them later, and I admired the cheerful ease with which they handled the discomforts of the climb. The father was a Protestant missionary from California, assigned to a post in Kenya. His daughters told us that they had been in Africa several years, with a few trips home. The girls were trim and pretty; the father jovial and heavy-set. He seemed more exuberant than organized, and I doubted he was prepared for what was ahead. The three were fixing their own breakfast and I did not see their porters.

The room soon filled up as other hikers appeared, including last night's diners. The latter were well rested, well organized and equipped, and in irritatingly good humor. I also saw the courteous Frenchman who was originally to join our group. He and his friends ate quickly and headed off.

About 8:00 we set out. Godwinn, Tom Jr.'s porter, had trouble tying a sleeping bag to the pack, and he and Tom Jr. were delayed. Effatta scolded them and, before they left, had Tom Jr. check the hut for any belongings our group might have left behind. The trail began in back of the main hut and led up into thick trees, moving along the side of a hill before turning west. The foliage was heavy and the most noticeable characteristic of this area, as indeed of the area below, was the profusion of long, strong vines. Although the trees looked much like those of the southeastern United States, they had an unfamiliar structure and texture. It was cloudy, threatening rain. A light jacket was all we needed, but as we moved up the hill it became too hot with a jacket, and too cool without one. We stayed together up the first hill as the trail followed a creek bed, but with switchbacks on the steeper parts. Other hikers had started out both ahead of and immediately behind us, but they all disappeared from view.

About an hour and a half above the Mandara Huts we came to the top of a small hill. The trees had thinned out and there was a comfortable grassy area with boulders to rest on. No one was tired, but it was an inviting place to pause. We took pictures and socialized as best we could across the language barrier. Several of the porters were smiling because some of us had given them caps. Tom G. loaned his porter a down jacket.

We moved along the side of a hill, the trees dropping off to the left. A broad area of grass and bushes stretched to the right. The clouds were heavy but the wind had increased, pushing them like large black ships across the sky. Then it cleared to the north and suddenly, looming up on top of us, were the ragged snow-covered spires of Mount Mawenzi. It looked like a celestial organ, and we paused, almost waiting for the music. The base of the mountain was still in clouds, but not long after they, too, blew by, and we had our first complete view of this rugged giant which reaches over 17,000 feet. We were at about 11,000 feet and the mountain, more than a mile farther in the sky, was so sharp and clear it seemed close enough to touch. At this point we could not see Kilimanjaro, which was still blocked by the shoulder hills to the west. Mawenzi, therefore, rearing up out of the green forest, was a striking sight. Pondering the fact that it was by no means as high as Kilimanjaro, I began to wonder, for the first time concretely, whether we were up to the challenge.

It began to drizzle and then to rain steadily. The porters were ahead, and it was so dark and cloudy that I could see nothing except the immediate trail. We had, without noticing it, moved above the tree line. But there were still bushes, some shoulder high.

Five of us were together: Tom Jr., John, and I in front, Stu and Tom G. behind. Effatta was somewhere farther back. As the rain pelted us, there was the urge to move faster, both to cover the distance and to keep warm. Tom G.'s foot was hurting, and he dropped back. When I inquired, John said Effatta would stay with him. I held slow. My poncho and rainpants kept out the rain, but my feet, even with the gaiters, were soaked and muddy. Repeatedly, some effort was required to avoid slipping.

There was no one coming down. On trails at home, when one starts to get discouraged, a returning hiker usually appears to drop an encouraging word. We saw no one.

The trail repeatedly peaked and fell but the grade was incessantly upward. Stu had generously but mistakenly carried his own pack and the altitude started to take its toll. We came to a drop where the trail crossed a stream; fed by the rain and the snow far above, the waters were crashing down. The rocky sides were an ideal resting place and a great opportunity to drink. Seated in the downpour, the four of us had a small lunch of roast beef sandwiches Felix had given us, together with our own peanuts and granola bars. We stretched out on the side of the gully, our hands shielding the bread from saturation from the rain. As the water ran down my face, I felt that exquisite relaxation that comes only from sustained exertion and could not resist comparing our situation to a story I'd read about Theodore Roosevelt. As a young man in the 1880s, he was hunting in South Dakota. His guide was a tough cowboy. They were on horseback all day, tracking a wounded bear, and were far from shelter as night fell. It rained heavily but they had no tent and could only wrap up in their blankets, shivering and miserable. Roosevelt, a small man with thick glasses, close-cut hair, and a squeaky voice, struck his guide as the quintessential Eastern effete. Years later, the guide told of his amazement when, lying in the dark, he heard Roosevelt muttering to himself, "By Godfrey but this is fun!"

Although we were above the tree line, where in clear weather the vistas to the south must be spectacular, I saw nothing but clouds, rain, and the monotonous mud of the trail. By midafternoon we reached a washboard series of small hills and valleys; after expecting at each rise that the Horombo Huts would come in sight, finally, after the third dip, we saw a hut on the hill above. From the angle of our approach I could not tell the layout, but as I climbed up the hill, I saw this was the main hut and that others, partly obscured in the mist, spread out behind and to the west on a large plateau.

We dragged up the steps of the main hut, intent on getting under cover. The inside was crowded, so I dumped my daypack near the stove at the back. None of our group was in sight. Some Japanese were coming down from the loft, and I climbed up to look there. The bunks were completely taken by Japanese hikers. We had been beaten to the loft the first night by the French and now we were beaten by the Japanese. This was the first time I had seen their large group, several of whom smiled in greeting as my head appeared in the loft.

I have long had a warm, if arm's-length, feeling for the ubiquitous, peripatetic, photomanic, courteous Japanese. It began for me over forty years ago, when I stood at the rail of an army transport and looked down on the Yokohama docks. The boys playing there grinned back with the toothy smiles of youth. They wore peculiar sneakers, which had a separate section for the big toe. The first Japanese I had ever seen, their spontaneous warmth immediately diluted my left-over reactions from the war. I was similarly taken by the Japanese girls we saw from our troop train as it moved south to Kyushu. As the train slowed or stopped passing through stations, GIs stretched out the windows and yelled outrageous if good-natured greetings; the girls huddled together bashfully and giggled.

The two Japanese I came to know best cemented these nascent feelings. I was headquartered in Kokura, a city at the top of Kyushu, where I edited the 24th Infantry Division newspaper. One of our interpreters was Noguchi San, then in his early thirties, a graduate of Tokyo University. He had been a lieutenant in the Japanese army, but had not served overseas. Noguchi was instinctively courteous and pleasant, if slightly delicate in manner. He had a round face, not atypical of the Japanese, and an open smile. For twelve months I worked with him daily. He took a lot of abuse from the GIs because, in an effort to please, he was overly deferential and, at the same time, understandably sensitive to being called a "gook," then a common GI term for anyone born west of the Golden Gate Bridge.

But Noguchi, even when he forgot to be obsequious, was genuinely friendly, happy, and courteous; his real colors, untouched, were true, and exactly what one would wish for in a friend and co-worker. Straightforward and interesting in serious conversation, he was the only Japanese to tell me his impressions of their propaganda and war news as events occurred. After Pearl Harbor and the Japanese victories in the Pacific, the public was given glowing accounts of the war. Confidence in ultimate victory was widespread. But Noguchi was sophisticated and well-informed; he realized from the beginning that only quick and extensive successes in the Pacific would give Japan any chance against the United States.

He remembered that in August 1942, after eight months of uninterrupted Japanese victories, came the unwelcome news that American marines had landed on the remote island of Guadalcanal. The landings were reported in Japan, but it was widely assumed this was only a prelude to the announcement that the landing forces had been wiped out. Noguchi recalled his concern as the weeks went by with scant further mention of Guadalcanal. He soon suspected that the Americans were holding, and were in fact going to capture the island. From then on, Noguchi said, he feared for the ultimate outcome.

Noguchi commuted to work—an unheard-of routine in those days—from the southern tip of Honshu, taking a train that passed under the Shimonoseki Straits, the ocean passage which connects Honshu and Kyushu. This took well over an hour each way. We were curious about Noguchi's home and family. He said his wife had been selected by his parents in consultation with hers, and that he had not seen her until just before they were married. We rudely inquired how he liked her when he was introduced, and he smiled broadly and said, "Very much, yes, very much." One afternoon his wife came to our office. She was beautiful, cultured, and refined. Compared to most of the working-class Japanese women who came within sight of the American soldiers, Noguchi's wife was a queen. Our respect for the taste of his parents reached high levels.

My other close Japanese friend was a little man named Arashi, who drew cartoons for our paper. He sat near me on a high stool at an artist's desk. Arashi was in every way the opposite of Noguchi: uneducated, sharp-featured, with a swagger in his walk. With his perky manner and mischievous expression, he might have been one of the seven dwarfs. Arashi had not been taught English but had nevertheless acquired, from American GIs, a workable vocabulary—mostly obscenities he practiced with vigor whenever he made a mistake in his drawing. He was also a natural acrobat. Pausing in his close work, he would get off his stool, flip up on his hands, walk across the floor up onto a chair, then onto one of the desks and proceed in this fashion around the room, grinning up at us. We would clap and cheer, his expression as captivating as his performance.

During the war Arashi had drawn Japanese propaganda posters. He redid for us some of the more extreme caricatures of heroic Japanese and shriveling Americans. He told us that in the later stages of the war American bombers could be heard regularly at night, as they flew over Kokura to targets on Honshu. They also bombed the Shimonoseki Straits continuously, trying to knock out the railroad tunnel that Noguchi now used to come to work. This tunnel was a vital link in the Japanese transportation system and the principal means of carrying troops and supplies south to Kyushu, where the American invasion was expected. The Americans, however, did not succeed in hitting the tunnel.

Although unknown to Arashi at the time, Kokura was one of the alternate targets for the second atomic bomb, the one that was dropped on Nagasaki. If there had been clouds over Nagasaki on August 9, 1945, Kokura instead would have been turned to dust. A year after I left Japan, Arashi wrote me a letter—friendly, interesting, and courteous. I am ashamed to say that back at college and caught up in my own affairs, I put it aside and never replied.

These two friendships produced a reservoir of good will that has remained undepleted through the years. Whenever I have encountered their countrymen, I have thought with a smile of these early friends. And in recent years their countrymen are often to be seen. A prosperous Japan has seemed to relieve crowding by maintaining a part of its population in constant circulation overseas. Whatever sights are worth seeing, the Japanese are seeing them; wherever it is worth being, they are there. One November—not the best tourist season—Mary Lee and I were at Saint Mark's Square in Venice; there were the Japanese, big signs raised so their group could be collected. One August night in Paris, in front of the Folies Bergère, when we were considering whether it was suitable to take in John and Peter, up pulled a busload of Japanese; out they tumbled, the men, cameras swinging from their necks, rushing expectantly into the show. The next morning we encountered the same group, properly somber, at Napoleon's tomb. Another summer, in the desert at Lone Pine, California, far from a tourist spot, a large bus stopped, discharging dozens of Japanese. It was, therefore, no surprise to find them on Kilimanjaro. Others were undoubtedly on Aconcagua, on the Matterhorn, even on Everest.

As I came back down the ladder I saw Tom. He told me we had one A-frame but would get another for the second night. The first was just in back of the main hut, and when I got there wet clothes were hanging everywhere; packs, hiking sticks and day packs filled the floor. It was shelter, however, and crowded together we would keep warm. We experimented to fit eight in the available space, proceeding on the principal that the oldest had first choice on the four bunks. I had the only upper bunk, at the back, with Tom underneath. Then I agreed to share my bunk with John, and we tested, lying with our heads at opposite ends. But the bunk was too narrow for two. Stu and Tom G. had not yet arrived but, as next oldest, were assigned the side bunks in absentia. The others squeezed together on the floor. We got pads from the caretaker and placed them between the side bunks, which were only inches above the floor. This made a single level where six cramped bodies would have to pass the night.

Some of us took naps. Others went into the main hut,

where Tom Jr. noticed the young girl from the previous day looking at John; they kidded him, but he professed loyalty to his girlfriend back home. Tired and wet, Stu and Tom G. finally arrived. Stu felt he needed a porter—his pack was becoming too much for him. He had also left his down jacket at the Mandara Huts. This could be a major problem higher up.

About 4:30, on schedule, Felix served tea and biscuits. As we sat at the table the two daughters of the missionary arrived, and a little later he too appeared. He was wrapped in a plastic covering, his hair was soaked, and water stood on his eyebrows. He bounded in shaking off the rain, exclaiming, "It's really wet out there; it's sure wet out there."

People were working at the stove at the rear. The mournful Canadian woman, whom I had not seen on the trail, asked if I would start a fire, adding, "There are some people who would appreciate it very much." Their porters had not arrived; they were feeling neglected and worried about getting dinner. As I stretched to put clothes on a string above the stove, the area like a tenement on wash day, I fell backward onto the brick base. This created a loud crash and stir in the hut, but I was not hurt.

The two Toms soon renewed their acquaintance with the Swiss family, particularly with the daughter, who, apparently with an eye to future possibilities, wanted to exchange addresses. Her name was Corin, and she and her boyfriend, Louis, were tree surgeons. Louis was leaving the next morning for Kibo Hut and the summit; she and her parents were turning back. Her father said he had been to the top twice and never had to go again. By 7:00 it was dark and most of us started back to the hut. Stu had found a group of Germans and spent the evening in language practice.

The rain continued during the night and was coming

down steadily when we awoke. This was a rest day, and it was wonderfully comfortable lying there with nothing to do. The Japanese were also taking the day off. I greeted some of them, exhausting my vocabulary in a moment of exchange. Only a few spoke English, none fluently. They were well-groomed, stylishly attired, and adorned with cameras.

John told me that the French-speaking group were not French but Belgian. They left in the rain, followed by others, including the missionary and his daughters. In a short time, the latter returned. The missionary said their guides had wanted to continue, but he'd decided it was too wet and made them turn back.

I asked one of the girls, who was about fifteen, where she went to school. She did not attend school but taught herself through a correspondence course, and had done so for several years. I assumed her father must be stationed in a remote area to require this expedient, and was curious to know how she had progressed. But I could not pursue the matter because near noon it began to blow clear and they left.

Also in the hut, an older Dutchman and a friend passed the afternoon playing chess on a small board. They were part of a family group which included his wife, daughter, and several friends, two of whom were ill in the loft. Disturbed, I asked how sick they were. The Dutchman replied they were not very sick and that he and his friend were both doctors, so not to worry. Tom and Stu each played chess with the doctors. I read a paperback copy of Freud's *Wit and Its Relation to the Unconscious.* Nearby were two American couples and two teenage children. The men worked for the U.S. Agency for International Development and were stationed in Kenya; the younger man had a guide book that described the Kilimanjaro trails, as well as the trails up Mount Kenya. He also had a contour map providing extensive detail on the route we were taking. The women were attractive and friendly.

In midafternoon the sun appeared. Heavy clouds blew by occasionally, many below us as we looked away to the south from the plateau. But the panorama soon widened. Nearby we could now see all the porters' huts and the entire level on which the Horombo Huts are located. A little later the winds cleared the clouds in the west, and there, for the first time, we saw in the distance the awesome summit of Kilimanjaro. It was blanketed with snow, unlike any picture we had seen or anything we had ever expected to climb. I pondered the fact that, in addition to being surprisingly far away, it was over a mile higher than our present elevation. We studied it for several minutes. "That may be too much for us," Stu said.

With the cheering sun, everyone was soon outside socializing and spreading clothes on the rocks to dry. We considered a walk up the trail but decided it was better to conserve our strength.

A couple in their late twenties arrived back from the Kibo Hut. They were the children of the Dutch doctor. Both were lean and tanned. Their climbing goggles had left white circles around their eyes; their legs were streaked with mud, and their boots wet. They were elated because early that morning, they had made Gillman's Point and the man and one of their guides had gone on to Uruhu. They were experienced climbers, and John told me they had crampons and ice axes. Later, other hikers returned from above, but most of them had not reached the summit. They had run into a blizzard and had sunk knee deep in snow; there was snow even on the Saddle. We heard negative comments. "Don't go in the snow"—"Good luck, I hope you have better weather"—or, "There is not enough oxygen to climb in the snow."

Eight members of a Swiss mountaineering club returned still later in the afternoon. They too had reached the top earlier that morning. I did not see their equipment, but they were clearly experienced mountaineers. One of them had become snow-blind, after losing his sunglasses near the summit, and had to be led down from the Kibo Hut. We talked to a Belgian woman who had turned back before the Kibo Hut because it was snowing hard and her son was vomiting. She said she had panicked, and now regretted not going on. Drinking our afternoon tea, we pondered these reports. No one provided much detail, but all emphasized that the slope of the summit cone was steep, and all said they had been nauseous. One remark of the young Dutchman troubled me. He said that the night before, trying to sleep at Kibo Hut, his pulse was 140. This seemed extraordinary for his age and condition. Otherwise, there was no hint of danger in anything we heard, the dominant theme being snow and the rigor of the climb.

At 6:00 the faithful Felix brought us dinner. Livingstone, whom I rarely saw, came in and gave me two small notebooks belonging to Effatta. One had pictures of groups that Effatta had taken up the mountain, and in both books climbers had written tributes to Effatta's skill. They were in English, Japanese, Swiss, German, and French. Here were expressions of gratitude from hikers of every race and nationality. By this time I'd realized that Effatta was an important figure among the guide fraternity. After dinner we met him outside the main hut and discussed our schedule. He stated that now that we were getting high, we should "ask Effatta, not others" whatever we needed to know. He spoke crisply and emphatically, and I judged that greater care would be taken to avoid any mishaps as we approached the most difficult part of the climb. Effatta said we would see how the weather was and, if we reached Gillman's Point, "we"—meaning he—would decide whether to try for Uruhu. Those with "bad" heads or stomachs would be taken down. We should have our packs ready at 6:00 A.M. so the porters could start for the Kibo Hut. Looking at Effatta as darkness descended, he seemed entirely in his element, with the right bearing, the right tone and attitude. He said *la la Missouri*—"sleep well"—in Swahili.

The sky was now entirely clear and the stars appeared like tiny spotlights. As we stood in front of the main hut, we could see distant lights below. *These must be the lights of Moshi,* I thought. It was a surprise to have this view of civilization after three days on the trail.

During the afternoon the younger four, except for Roland, who stayed with us, had moved into an adjoining hut. We were therefore in comparative luxury. After a day of rest and the confidence that came from our chat with Effatta, we were as ready as I could have hoped for what lay ahead.

Stu, Tom G., Tom, John, Tom Jr., the author, Roland, and Peter at the Kibo Hotel

The Mandara Huts

Mandara Huts breakfast—Tom, John, and the author

John, the author, and Peter at the Horombo Huts

Chapter 10
The Kibo Hut

I awoke before daylight and went outside. The stars were still spectacular and the weather had finally cleared for good. A gray tinge developed in the east and soon it was daylight. The porters picked up our packs and a few of them left immediately. At 6:30 we had eggs, porridge, bread, and tea. The area outside was bustling, and the temperature was rising quickly with the sun. Everyone was cheerful and eager. We took pictures outside the huts, the summit in the distance. It was still intimidating and even more beautiful in the sunlight. I looked over and saw Effatta giving instructions to Livingstone, who ran off to one of the other huts. He was certainly jumping to it, considering we were at 12,500 feet.

A string of porters were now moving up the hill toward Kilimanjaro, red, green, and blue packs dotting the distant slope. We set off, Stu having lightened his pack by putting clothes in those carried by the porters. Ahead of us was the large Japanese group, the four Frenchmen from the Kibo Hotel, and two or three other parties that I had not previously seen. A beautiful English woman and a less attractive friend went quickly past us; they, however, were merely checking the trail for a short distance and were not starting up until the next day. Someone said the Canadian couple and their companion had turned back.

Except for the giant groundsels, of which there were astonishing examples at this elevation, the vegetation was diminishing, and the ever-smaller bushes were dry and brittle. There were no birds or other wildlife. Most of the Japanese group was in front of us but several of the men, who must have started late, hurried past. A hundred yards later we caught up as they rested; then they rushed by again. The same thing occurred with the Frenchmen, one of whom had large muscular calves. Within two hours, however, we came upon the Frenchmen resting; one was sick and they had decided to give up. It was too bad, after they'd expended four days' effort to reach this point. The Japanese continued their fit-and-start routine, clicking pictures along the way. An older Japanese, who moved at a steady pace, branched off on side excursions and twisted himself in various positions to get closeups of the groundsels.

The sun was hot. We had covered our faces with lotion and put scarves over the backs of our necks. Peter knocked one of the lenses from his sunglasses, which would be essential on the summit cone. Fortunately, he managed to fit the lens back in place.

As one moves above 13,000 feet, the thinning atmosphere does little to filter ultraviolet rays. And at the equator they are coming almost straight down, rather than, as in temperate climes, on a slant. The latter problem is reduced somewhat in late December, the rays at the equator being then on more of a slant than on March 21 or September 21, when the sun is overhead. Nonetheless, they are still quite direct.

As the trail rose westward, we reached a point entirely above the hills that until then had partially surrounded us; now the vistas opened in all directions except to the west, where the shoulder of the mountain still cut off all but the summit. Mawenzi came into full view on the north, looking less imposing than before. Its ragged spires reached upward, but there was only light snow on the approaches. The trail soon split in several directions, and we started tentatively on the one that appeared correct. But we were mistaken. Looking back we finally saw Effatta who signalled the right way; we retraced our steps, costing energy. At the top of another hill, Effatta caught up with me and we rested. He began to gather pieces of dry brush. Some of the porters for the Japanese group passed, brush packets also tied to their loads. I wondered what other preparations were underway for the conditions above.

At noon we reached the top of another rise and had our first view of the Saddle. Other than the sandy color, it resembled the moon and would have been a perfect training ground for astronauts. The Japanese were having lunch, and we also paused to eat. I gave Effatta peanuts, and we took pictures. For the first time I noticed his cane, which was light and without a steel tip. It had a brass plate near the top, which I took to indicate his status as a guide. Later I had the impression that the head guides carried canes instead of sticks and that the canes were more ornamental than useful. The other guides and the porters had neither canes nor sticks.

The trail descended to a soggy pasture and a stream. A wooden sign said "Last Water." The Japanese and a few other hikers were taking pictures and filling canteens. We did the same and then proceeded to a rocky ridge, which drops down to the Saddle. At the top of the ridge we had our first view of the whole summit cone. It was snow-covered all the way to the base, the snow extending onto the contiguous portions of the Saddle. The Saddle, several miles across on the route we would take, was littered with rocks tossed out eons ago by the volcanic eruptions that created Kilimanjaro and Mawenzi. Both were now fully visible. The comparison was startling. Although not jagged and only a half-mile higher, Kilimanjaro's enormous bulk completely dwarfed Mawenzi.

The summit did not seem far away at this point, and

the walk across the Saddle, which rises steadily but gently, appeared an easy stroll. But Neil had warned me that he had set off here at a normal pace, and was soon exhausted from the altitude and the deceptive grade. The trail dropped onto the Saddle at 13,500 feet and we would be moving up 2,000 feet higher before we reached the Kibo Hut. Our porters and the Japanese party started ahead. We watched as they dwindled in size and were swallowed up by the vastness of the Saddle, although it all seemed plainly in view.

Moving slowly across the Saddle on a sunny day was a nice change from the trees and shrubs below. We passed a few porters, returning from the Kibo Hut, but no hikers during the first two hours. It was now early afternoon and we rested often, stretching out on the ground. Stu, despite his lightened pack, still carried more than the others. He lay on the dry ground with his hat over his face as if down for the count. We looked forward and backward and, except for the two mountains, could distinguish nothing in any direction.

When we were more than halfway across the Saddle and beginning to turn north toward the lower shoulder of the summit cone, I saw a porter approaching. Not far behind him came the missionary.

"How did you make out?" I inquired.

"Wow, it was more than I bargained for."

Pointing his stick toward a black line in the snow of the summit cone—a line that had just come into view—he said, "That's your route to the top, that's the route you'll have to take." The line he was indicating looked impossibly steep.

"You should have a couple of sticks for coming down. It's slippery and you could get killed up there. One fellow slid and went 'whoosh.' If he hadn't stopped on some rocks, he'd have gone all the way. I made my daughters stop at the cave because I was worried that they'd be hit by rocks; you can't even see them until it's too late. I've been up to 21,000 before, but it wasn't like this. But everything worked out. Have a good time."

Then he hustled on, calling back, "If you see my daughters, tell them to hurry."

I was amazed that this fellow had reached the top and was already on his way back—ahead of everyone else, including the Belgians. Probably he lived at a high elevation in Kenya. Still, it was good to know that this jovial, overweight, middle-aged missionary could make it to the top. Soon came his daughters, fresh and cheerful as ever. We gave them the word to hurry. "We will, we will," they assured us and waved good-bye.

As we approached the base of the summit cone, I saw a glare in the rocks ahead and made it out to be the roof of the Kibo Hut. It was a pinhead among the boulders that cover the eastern base of the cone. Soon the glare disappeared, hidden by the hill of rocks ahead. Snow patches began to appear around us, increasing in size as we moved up until snow covered the ground. The Swedish woman and her two children were sitting on a rock, and we stopped to chat. They had decided that this was as far as they would go, and were ready to start back to the Horombo Huts for the night. Farther on, we began to meet the first of the returning Belgians. The afternoon was getting on and I thought it late for them to be this far up, but they seemed in no hurry. A few looked bedraggled, but most were in good condition. One told John that half of them had reached the summit. As each one passed, we kept asking, "How was it?" but from their cryptic replies I suspected that most had not really gotten to the top. No one mentioned any special problems or danger, and the missionary's caution began to seem less important.

As we rounded one area of rocks, the Kibo Hut appeared ahead, up a steep rise. I was barely moving, fully protected by gloves, glasses, and a sun hat, with a flap down the back of my neck. As I got closer I could see some of our porters stretched on the rocks. Livingstone came down to take my day pack; I kept only my movie camera to take shots of the others coming up. Stu was not far behind me, carrying his own pack. In my relief at handing Livingstone my day pack I did not think of Stu, who was more deserving of relief. He said nothing and proceeded on. As they came up the trail my movie camera caught Tom and his sons; they and others behind them appeared to be moving with an exaggerated slowness, as if I had reduced the speed of the film.

There are two buildings at the Kibo Hut. The one for hikers is made of stone, and is set parallel to the side of the hill. It has a corridor running through the center, with two bunk rooms off each side. The Japanese already occupied three. The other room was assigned to us and the Americans from Nairobi, who were unpacking their gear when we entered. At the end of the corridor is another room, intended as a general eating area; it was being used by two couples who had pitched a tent outside. One wonders how the cement and other equipment necessary for the construction of this building were brought to this altitude. The building, like the huts below, was built in the early 1970s as part of a Norwegian aid project.

Having outdistanced most of those who, with equally fond hopes, had left the Gate four days before, and with the Belgian group having departed, we now enjoyed our best accommodations to date. Our room had six pairs of double-decker bunks, and a window across the top of the side facing the mountain. Beneath the windows were two tables with benches.

The sun was now in the west, over the summit, so we could not get pictures of the face of the mountain. By shading our eyes with our hands, however, we could see it clearly. It was a gigantic wall of snow, stretching up over two miles to the top.

North of the hikers' hut was another stone building where the porters cooked and slept. Down a small slope in the other direction was an outhouse, but reaching it and then returning took so much energy that it was used only as a last resort.

We settled down to rest, Peter testing an aluminum emergency blanket. Everyone looked pale. But we were in good spirits, except that Stu felt sick. After a short rest we went outside to take pictures. The air was cool but pleasant. About 5:00, Fred and Felix came in with tea and biscuits, followed, for the first time on these occasions, by Effatta. He said we would sleep from 6:00 until 1:00 A.M. when we would start for the summit. We were to pack our gear for the return trip and leave it in our bunk so that the porters could pick up our packs as soon as we came down; we would then have them at the Horombo Huts that night. I debated taking my day pack to the summit but decided against carrying anything I could not put in my pockets. Every moment in preparation took twice as long at this altitude, but in half an hour we were ready to try to sleep.

When we were chatting with the other Americans they said they had taken Diamox pills, prescribed by an American physician in Nairobi. They thought it would help on their way to the summit. They had extra pills and offered them to us. In retrospect it seems rash to have accepted this offer, but we had seen these people enough in recent days to feel that they were reliable, and I knew from Dr.

Houston that Diamox might help. They said that they had all taken the pills each of the last two days with no ill effects, and were now taking them again. We did the same. Whether for that or other reasons we all slept well, although Diamox is a diuretic and I had to get up twice during the night. Both times Stu came out too, and we laughed as we stood looking up at the stars. Just before I went to sleep, I took my pulse. It was only seventy beats per minute, about ten to twelve more than my resting pulse at sea level. This was a good sign.

Effatta Jonathan near the "Last Water"

Tom G. and Stu at the edge of the Saddle

Crossing the Saddle: Tom Jr. standing; Tom G. and Peter seated; Stu and Tom prostrate

Kibo Hut: Roland, Tom, Tom Jr., the author, and John

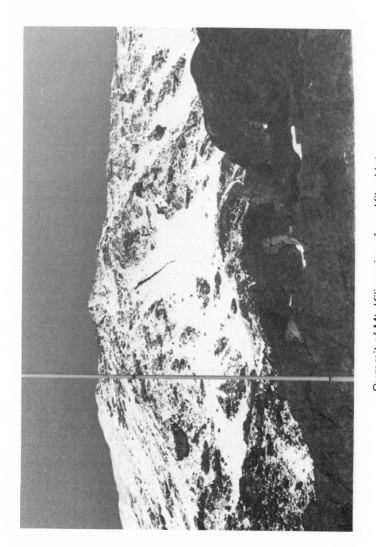

Summit of Mt. Kilimanjaro from Kibo Hut

Chapter 11
Zanzibar and Dar es Salaam

When they left the Kibo Hotel, the women looked forward to an exotic adventure of their own. The remote island of Zanzibar awaited them. Less than a century ago it was the lair of the Arab slavetraders, who from here had launched their savage expeditions into the interior. Today it boasted a resort hotel looking out on the azure sea. The travel brochure provided this description of the Oberoi Ya Bwawani Hotel:

> MODERN FIRST CLASS HOTEL facing the Indian Ocean, twenty minutes from seaport or airport. Large tastefully decorated rooms with air conditioning, bath, telephone, color TV and balcony. Rooftop restaurant and American-style coffee shop. Two bars and discotheque. Large salt water pool/water sports.

Its cruel history in the faded past, Zanzibar promised the elegance of a Caribbean retreat.

The flight to Dar es Salaam was scheduled for 11:00 A.M., but when the travelers reached the ticket counter they learned that "the plane has been discontinued. Not to worry," the clerk assured them, "another will appear, soon." Glad not to have paid on Sunday for a phantom flight, especially without a receipt, the women resigned themselves to waiting skeptically. An hour later, a plane did appear. It was a comfortably familiar DC-9, sporting perkily uniformed stewardesses. As they took off, Ellen was disappointed that bad weather on Kilimanjaro still prevented getting pictures of the summit.

Climbing rapidly, the plane reached cruising altitude.

Mary Lee and Alice sat together; Ellen and Linda were across the aisle. The stewardesses served pineapple juice, and Mary Lee, feeling better, sipped it cautiously. Linda lit a cigarette.

There was suddenly a loud, suctionlike hiss of air. Mary Lee gripped Alice's arm; an Indian mother in the seat ahead threw her arms around her children; a stewardess raced down the aisle; the powerful rush of air grew louder. Linda thought her heart stopped; she remembered a movie where the door blew off and a man was sucked into space. Ellen thought, *We are going down; it is all because we had a bad start. But I'm laughing, so I have a sense of humor, even if we are going into the Indian Ocean.* Alice felt, *We are done for. It's not so bad to crash. I'm not panicking. Tom's going to feel really bad for letting us go off alone.*

Mary Lee, just starting to feel well, looked back; a yellow life raft was inflating inside the plane, passengers scrambling from their seats as it enveloped them. Two more stewardesses, laughing, ran to help as the raft expanded in the back of the plane. Seeing the doors still closed and feeling the plane steady, the passengers realized that the raft was the culprit. They settled back, exhausted.

An hour later they landed peacefully in Dar es Salaam. A representative from the Tourist Office who was to meet them at the airport was nowhere in sight. On directions from Air Tanzania, the travelers went to an adjoining terminal for the smaller aircraft to Zanzibar. Crowds packed the interior of the building as, like two pairs of dice in a black sea, the women worked their way to the ticket counter. Here in a swell of steaming humanity were the tribes and races of Africa and Arabia; women, hooded and masked, in flowing gowns and purdahs; bearded men with untouched hair, wearing black, white, and red turbans.

106

Baggage and sacks of every kind, baskets of clothes and other impedimenta covered the floor. The four white women caused the black sea to part, and they passed through to the ticket counter where they explained that they were on the 1:35 P.M. flight to Zanzibar.

"Sorry, you are not on the list," explained the clerk after checking the roster.

"But we are prepaid and these reservations were made by the Tourist Office."

"I can do nothing. You had better check with them," the clerk replied.

Alice and Linda called Mr. Lilla's local assistant, Miss Marion Islem, who was to have met them on arrival. A half hour later she appeared, the women wilting in the heat of the crowded building. She took them to the airport manager, who had the only air-conditioned room. In reply to their protests and to Ellen's repeated assertion that "my sister, she is sick," he assured them, "It's okay, ladies; it's okay," and made them reservations on the next Zanzibar flight, leaving two hours later. In the interim, they would have rooms at the Kilimanjaro Hotel, which the Tourist Office operated, and lunch in the roof dining area.

The shaded roof offered limited relief from the blanket of heat that has a permanent clamp on Dar es Salaam. After sipping soup, Mary Lee went to her room to rest. The others ordered seafood and chicken newburg, which some Indian women were eating. Waiting in the lobby for the van to return them to the airport, Linda saw a beautiful picture of the Hotel Bwawani. On the way to the airport, the driver inquired if they wanted to buy shillings for U.S. dollars, asking them to promise that they would not report him to the Tourist Office. Having already had trouble enough, the women declined.

The terminal building was again oppressively hot, and

Ellen demanded a wheelchair for Mary Lee. With this distinguishing accoutrement, the travelers, in the style of a sultan's wives, pushed through the throng to the small prop plane for Zanzibar.

Miss Islem had called ahead and a Tourist Office man met them when they landed. As they entered the terminal, the government agent took their passports and asked for their yellow-fever certificates. "What certificates? No one mentioned certificates." "No entry without certificates," he explained.

Ellen, who is not large but can be formidable, replied with now-practiced emphasis, "My sister, she is sick," frowning as if further annoyances would produce unspecified repercussions. At the same time she noticed the Tourist Office man pulling papers from an inside pocket, and suspected these were backup documents to be tendered as yellow-fever certificates. The government agent, intimidated by Ellen's attitude, waved them through without more discussion. But he retained the passports, saying they could be retrieved the next day at the Tourist Office.

Outside, a driver approached, urging that they sign up for an island tour which included the spice groves, Livingstone's home, native huts, and the ruins of the Sultan's palace. Alice and Linda—with visions of the hotel—were not interested. But learning that it would cost the same for two as for four, they cooperatively agreed to share the expense. For $100, the driver would carry them between hotel and airport now and when they left, and the next day would take them on tour.

Leaving the airport one could see in the distance, on the edge of town, drab apartment buildings of gray cement, six or eight stories high, strikingly unsuited to the sunny African environment. Harry, the driver, said they had been built by the East Germans. Overcrowding and the mildew from a constant humidity had turned them into slums. Wash covered the railings of the balconies.

The cab did not go into town, the hotel being on a strip of land between the ocean and, as it soon appeared, a mosquito-breeding marsh. The building was large, pitted and peeling—the coup de grace to the illusion of a sparkling resort. Built only ten years earlier by a revolutionary leader whose statue stood between the hotel and the ocean, it was already dirty and discolored, like a wrecked yacht battered by sun and sea. Inside, a thick red entrance hall carpet, more appropriate for the climates of Europe, reeked of mildew. The front desk maintained a faded dignity, but the rooms were dirty and mildewed as well. There appeared to be only a few other guests in accommodations built for hundreds. A couple with two children, perhaps Australians, had just arrived; they looked similarly disconcerted.

Alice and Linda's room had a dismal inland view. Mary Lee and Ellen's faced the ocean but the vista was not much better. The beach was dirt and weeds, a salty swamp stretching fifty yards till it gave way to deeper water. The bay was dark, without movement. A few scows and barges rested at anchor, but even commercial shipping seemed to have sought less depressing harbors.

Both rooms hummed with mosquitoes, the bedclothes were soggy, and the TV sets broken. To revive their spirits, the women unpacked quickly and set off to look for the pool. Off the first floor veranda they came upon a gray cylindrical building with a "Disco" sign. Beyond it, there was a deck and perhaps a pool. But the only entrance was through the building and the doorway was blocked by a chain long in place. Returning to the main lobby, they inquired at the registration desk. The clerk shook her head; the pool was "closed up."

The women tried calling other hotels, but could not get through. They went back to the room clerk who said she had no ocean-side rooms with screens; when the women protested that they had seen many on their walk outside, the clerk explained that these were on floors that had been "closed off." She promised, however, that when the women were at dinner, Mary Lee's and Ellen's bags would be moved across the hall to a room with screens and that DDT bombs would be set off in both rooms.

An open, airy dining hall was the hotel's single saving feature, but the women decided that moving the next day was the top priority. When they reached the elevator on the way back to their rooms, a strong DDT odor met them from above.

Harry appeared the next morning. He was upset to hear their problems with the hotel and said he would show them the "second best" hotel in town. He would also take them to the tourist office if they wanted to arrange a flight out. His concern was endearing. Harry had a red cab, with animal skins covering the seats and good luck charms hanging from the ceiling. He was proud of his vehicle, which was clean and neat. His cheerful, helpful attitude gave them a lift.

The town itself had a charm missing on the outskirts. Pastel buildings with columns flanked the streets, and women with multicolored dresses carried baskets on their heads. Harry steered expertly through the crowded streets, finally stopping before a building with a broad, open stairway leading to the entrance. "Second best, cleanest hotel in town," he announced, and Ellen saw that it was indeed mentioned in a guidebook to historic buildings. But the lobby was small and gloomy, with a bare floor and a few wooden chairs. At one table three Indian women were drinking tea. No one was at the desk. It was obvious that changing hotels would be no improvement. A woman appeared and asked if they would like to see rooms, but they declined. Still trying, Harry took them to a rooming house near the waterfront. It had an open courtyard but dismal dormitory-type rooms.

Giving up, they went to the airline office. Three lines of Biblical characters stretched from inside the entrance into the street. In shifts, one in line and three on the side, they waited their turn amid the impressive odors. When they reached the reservation desk, the clerk, scanning pages of names, said theirs were not on the list for departure on the thirty-first or any other day, and that it would be impossible for them to leave until January 10. Showing their tickets had no effect. It seemed that, despite the union of Zanzibar and the mainland, there was some tension between them and even between airline offices. The clerk referred them to another desk where they might find out how to get a boat to the mainland. Again, a long wait in line; then, the second clerk said: "You might go to the harbor and try to hire someone to take you by water, but I doubt if you'll have any luck. There is a shortage of fuel for the boats. There have been dozens of ships on the perimeter of the harbor for weeks but those here lack fuel and cannot move out, blocking others from entering. There is also a shortage of aviation fuel, which is why there are so few flights."

Cast now in the role of refugees, the women headed quickly for the Tourist Office, Harry patiently encouraging. There a thin, smiling man said he would try to arrange a flight out the next day. It could not be done while they waited but "no problem"; he would come by the hotel that evening to let them know whether he had been successful. In the meantime, they should take their tour of the island. So, off they went in Harry's cab, first insisting that they go to the government office and try to negotiate the return of their passports. There they were told the passports were still at the airport and would not be brought in until later in the day. When they asked why the passports had been taken, the official whispered, "No reason." Later, they heard that the practice of passport collection had been in effect for only two weeks, since tensions had increased with the mainland.

Entering the older part of town, the cab moved through twisted streets, a car width in many places, people backing against the buildings to let it pass. These were the streets of the Arab traders of long ago. The cab came to a stop. A knurled, wizened man with a white Muslim skullcap, Gandhi-like shroud wrapped around his shoulders and pulled between his legs, wearing sandals and holding a staff—a relic worthy of Carbon 14 analysis—asked with a toothless smile if he could guide them on a walk through the narrow alleys. Harry explained that if the women wanted to see the oldest part of town, it could only be done on foot and with such a guide, whom Harry knew. But feeling they were already at the end of the earth, they decided against a walk through close streets, into strange, dirty, and perhaps risky places. With exaggerated politeness they declined.

Mary Lee asked Harry if she could find ivory and he took them down a side street, stopping before a small shop. Inside were ivory trinkets and carvings of all descriptions. The proprietor was a European in his sixties, his face tanned and wrinkled. He came over immediately, offering "a very good rate" for one hundred American dollars, because "I need them to get to Vienna; I must get out of here." His strained tone and manner disturbed them, anxious as they were about being stranded themselves. Mary Lee explained she did not want to change dollars; looking

112

discouraged, he did not press her. She bought several pieces of carved ivory, bargaining him down on some items to half his original price.

As they headed out of town Harry pointed out the Russian Consulate, a plain square building with the flag in front. Nearby was the former U.S. Consulate. It was now closed, and the building was being used as a yellow-fever research center. They passed a large domed building fronted with heavy columns. It had been a sultan's palace and was now used for offices. On the edge of town, over-looking the water, was a two-story pink house, a cement wall surrounding the front garden. A plaque stated it was the home of Livingstone in the years before his famous journeys to the interior.

They were soon away from town, the road winding through thick foliage, broken often by open patches in which huts of mud over stick skeletons, with straw roofs of woven leaves, were in various stages of construction. At one site people were bush weaving and building. Harry explained that friends and relatives were helping a newly married couple construct a shelter. They waved at the cab. Harry stopped and several children approached. He said to give them a Tanzanian penny or two—no more—and they would climb a tree to bring down a nutmeg. This they did with dexterity and a smile. Harry cut open the fruit, extracting the core, which had a strong nutmeg smell. Near other houses, in fenced-off areas, water buffalo grazed, white herons on their backs. Soon the road dwindled to a dirt trail, with the jungle trying to close over it. Although there seemed to be no organized planting, Harry knew where to stop: first, breaking off some leaves which he then separated, producing a coffee odor; farther, pulling down thick buds which he cut open, filling the air with the heavy scent of an African perfume. Several other varieties of spices and perfumes he exhibited, all mysteriously located amid the profusion of bushes and trees. On the trip back, they turned down a long straight road that had been the entrance drive to the Sultan's Palace; the consuming tropical vegetation had made the palace a Roman ruin. The stubs of large pillars stood like the rooks of a giant's chess set scattered in the overgrowth. Ledges of circular stone, which once framed a large entrance pool, now enclosed dirt and bushes. A few boys played on the rocks. Behind was a walkway, its roofless columns silent witnesses to an indulgent past.

As they neared town, Harry apologized as the unsightly apartments came into view. "This was a beautiful island before the Germans came and built those buildings, trying to move people from their huts. There was no need. They were happy, they did not need to work. Their food dropped from the trees." The women had indeed been impressed with the bright-looking people and their friendly waves as they stood in front of their mud huts.

Retrieving their passports at the Tourist Office, the women learned that no progress had been made with the airlines. The smiling man insisted he was working on it and promised to drop by the hotel later to report. When they returned to the hotel, tea was being served in the lounge.

Dinner produced a feeling of normalcy. Three German businessmen, later joined by an African, were seated nearby. There was one other couple and the Australian family. Part of the room was roped off because rain had come in through the windows, and plastic awnings had been lowered on the harbor side, which was open to the sea. Two cats—appearing to be a cross between Egyptian and Siamese—were walking on the rafters above the dining room. Alice, after getting the right word from the waiter, called to the cats in Swahili, but without success.

The menu was extensive. But as selections were made, the waiter in most cases reported, "That is finished." Eventually, an order was agreed on. The women were sipping government-brand beer and "double cola" when the man from the Tourist Office appeared. "I do not have reservations yet but everything will be fine. Don't worry. I came to reassure you." They wondered that he had not simply called. But dependent on him, they asked if he would stay for dinner. He declined dinner but accepted beer, and, sitting at the end with Mary Lee and Ellen on either side, proceeded to chat pleasantly. He had been to school in England, was in his thirties, married, and with two children. His family lived on the mainland, and he got home only twice a month. Mary Lee made conversation by asking about Zanzibar and the government, curious to know the extent of communist influence. He shunned political comment. Otherwise, he was polite and responsive, and took care to emphasize how expensive it was to bring things to Zanzibar.

During the night Mary Lee dreamed a man had come into the room and was trying to grab Ellen. Ellen heard her moaning and awakened her, saying "It's all right, everything's all right." She noticed that Mary Lee, despite the heat, was covered with goose pimples.

There was no word from the Tourist Office when they finished breakfast and returned to their rooms, Mary Lee to change to a cooler blouse. It was then she saw that a rash now covered her neck and chest. With sensitive skin, she assumed it was from the heat. Ellen was startled at the extent of the outbreak, which she could see also covered Mary Lee's back. Hiding her alarm, she said she was going to the lobby and would be back shortly.

The desk clerk told her there was a doctor in the adjoining building, which could be reached through the courtyard at the side of the hotel. Entering the building, Ellen saw she was in a bakery; on her left were hot ovens, and flour covered the floor. Following the hotel clerk's directions, she went to the second floor and down a long inside hallway. Offices were on either side. Most were closed, but some dark heads could be seen in a few that were open. In a room at the far end of the hall she found an old woman in a sari sitting at a desk. She was alone and spoke no English, but when Ellen got across that she sought a doctor, the woman indicated that the doctor was available in a room at the back.

Returning with Mary Lee, who was impressed that Ellen had ventured into such surroundings, they discovered the doctor to be a European-educated Indian woman. She was dressed in a white coat and seated at a desk. Her examining room had a leather-covered medical table. Behind it, along the wall, were rows of whiskey bottles.

A glance and the doctor told Mary Lee, "I think it's an allergic reaction." She reached below to a desk drawer and, without raising up, could be heard to pour some tablets into a cup she fashioned out of newspaper. "This is antihistamine," she said, "take two every four hours." Ellen explained they hoped to be returning to the mainland and then to Arusha, whereupon the doctor wrote out the name and address of her niece in Arusha and asked them to look her up. She declined, with a smile, any charge for the visit.

By the time they got to their room Mary Lee was becoming faint from the medicine or the developing rash. She could think only of lying down. The others took turns watching her. She was not aware of the good news when it came: the Tourist Office man had gotten them on a plane, due to leave later that afternoon! As the time approached, they went to the lobby to wait. "Rest in the room," Ellen suggested, but Mary Lee did not want to be left alone and went down and stretched out on a sofa near the hotel entrance.

Harry arrived with the man from the Tourist Office and drove them to the airport. The terminal was a swarming mass of humanity. Alice and Linda got help for the luggage, and Mary Lee saw Ellen swallowed up in the crowd as she went with the tickets to check in and look for a wheelchair. An airline employee, spying Ellen, grasped her hand and pulled her through to the counter; hearing Mary Lee's condition, he found a wheelchair and brought it to her. In the meantime, the Tourist Office man was trying to make his way to the ticket counter. Ellen, looking at the long line ahead of him and determined not to have to return to the hotel, handed him $50. Taking the money, the Tourist Office man climbed the railing for a flank assault on the ticket counter. With Mary Lee hunched in the wheelchair, a wide hat covering the rash that had now spread over her face and which they feared might cause her to be barred from the plane, they waited anxiously. Shortly, the Tourist Office man appeared. "All set," he smiled, "don't say anything. Follow me." With that they moved through the crowd, Ellen pushing the wheelchair, Alice and Linda with the luggage. As they were cleared through into the waiting room, they waved thanks to the Tourist Office man who was soon inundated by the pushing crowd.

"How much did you give him?" Alice asked Ellen once they were seated in the area reserved for those with tickets. "Fifty," replied Ellen, "and I would have given him a hundred if I had to." Alice reached in her purse for half.

Mary Lee deteriorated as they helped her out onto the steaming landing strip and up the steps of the plane. She was conscious but unfocused on the flight to Dar es Salaam and during the ride to the hotel. The hotel, having no doctor, suggested they call a nearby clinic. A doctor there said they should come right over. The four women took a cab to the clinic, a gray building on a side street. Inside, a man at the desk told them to have a seat on one of the benches. There were four or five other patients, two with open sores, waiting. The room reeked of sulfur.

The doctor and a younger attendant were either Indians or Arabs. One look and the doctor pronounced that Mary Lee had a skin infection. "But the doctor in Zanzibar said I had an allergic reaction," she responded.

"Not at all. It's a skin infection. I'll give you a shot of penicillin, and you'll have to have shots at four-hour intervals. We are in short supply. I'll give you a prescription and you can try to find some at a chemist. Then you can bring it back here."

With that, a woman in white appeared with a tray and needle. Ellen had seen her take the needle from an uncovered tray in the next room and, in the friendliest tone, asked, "Are your needles sterile?"

This produced an angry reaction from the doctor. "Of course they're sterile. I have relatives in the States who are medical doctors; I visit the States often and bring back medicine. You Americans think you know everything."

The woman in white then filled the needle and, while the doctor and his male attendant modestly looked away, gave Mary Lee a shot in the seat.

Leaving the clinic with a prescription, they found a taxi driver who took them to a chemist, a small store with no sign or other identification. But it had no penicillin. Stops at three more chemists were equally futile. The stifling streets were teeming with people and the cab driver was constantly calling to friends. While the cab was stopped by the crowds, the doctor's assistant walked by. Looking in at Mary Lee, she smiled and said proudly to a friend, "She is my patient." There were a few white people on the streets;

118

they looked pale from the heat. Mary Lee was too weak to continue the search and they returned to the hotel and telephoned the doctor. He said to come back at 6:00 P.M. Mary Lee was dehydrated and tried ginger ale before attempting to sleep. Alice and Linda, determined to salvage some of the "vacation," went for a swim in the hotel pool.

With the uninviting prospect of returning to the clinic again at 6:00, and then at four-hour intervals through the night, the women decided on shifts and, for the first visit, Linda accompanied Mary Lee. They were met with a jolly greeting from a huge African woman in a navy-blue dress and white turban, possibly the uniform for Tanzanian nurses. She led them into the examining room, pointing to a cot for Mary Lee. Seeing the dirty sheets, however, Mary Lee decided to stand. The nurse said again and again, "How brave you are," laughing each time and compensating for the surroundings by her good-natured reassurance. Nonetheless, when she left to get a needle, Mary Lee cautioned Linda against sitting on the examining table, which had a leather covering through the splits of which the stuffing spilled out. Linda smiled encouragingly, "Now, Mary Lee, you hang on, everything will be fine."

When the nurse returned, ready with the injection, Mary Lee stood grasping the door jamb. As the needle went in, the point seemed to slice a nerve. When it was withdrawn, she dropped onto a wooden chair. The nurse with a wide smile exclaimed, "You're so brave; you're so brave."

It was dark when they came out and the street was empty. "Wait at the door," Linda said, and without hesitation set off up the street. Mary Lee watched her disappear around a corner. Soon a cab appeared, Linda in the back seat. Leaning out with a smile, she helped Mary Lee in.

Mary Lee became increasingly dehydrated. The others decided that it was too dangerous for only two to visit the clinic at night and they would all go together, but within a few hours Mary Lee had developed a fever and was too ill to move. The rash covered her body and the hot, wet, inescapable air was turning the sores to blisters, which stung with the constant perspiration. Before leaving Scarsdale, Mary Lee had asked at the drugstore for unbreakable traveler's thermometers. Now she discovered the clerk had given her only thermometer casings; there was no way to find out how high her fever had risen. Linda called the clinic to say that they could not come back and asked if a doctor might be sent; the jolly nurse checked and said another doctor and nurse would be sent to the hotel. In the meantime Ellen tried, without success, to reach Mary Lee's doctor in Scarsdale. She got through to the Scarsdale drugstore, however, and Mary Lee took the phone and asked to speak to the pharmacist, explaining that she was calling from Africa. It was now 10:00 P.M. in Dar es Salaam, but eight hours earlier in New York.

"Just a moment," said the girl at the drugstore. But it was more than a moment, and the minutes ticked by over the open line running halfway around the world before the pharmacist picked up the phone. Mary Lee explained which medicines she had taken, reading the labels off the bottles, and how the rash and fever had developed, urgently inquiring whether an allergic reaction might have occurred and what could be done. The pharmacist was unaware of any likely reaction, other than that exposure to the sun when taking antibiotics, such as the diarrhea medicine, sometimes produced a rash.

The doctor and nurse from the clinic then arrived. Mary Lee's fever was 102 degrees; they advised taking her immediately to the hospital. But schooled in the Arab's excessive concern with covering a woman's body, the doctor did not want to look at the rash or otherwise examine her. The African nurse, intelligent and practical, urged going to the hospital and reassured her, saying she had seen another white woman with a similar rash who after being hospitalized two or three days had "recovered nicely." While this discussion continued, Ellen reached our doctor in Scarsdale. He said to take Mary Lee to the hospital and there should be no problem as long as the conditions were clean and the needles sterile. Ellen said she was sure they were not. He then spoke at length with the clinic doctor and again told Ellen that he thought Mary Lee should be taken to the hospital. But Ellen and Mary Lee, remembering the dirty clinic linen, were not convinced. The fever and rash, the heat and humidity, and the strain of uncertainty, were now taking their toll. Mary Lee sensed she was seriously ill and getting worse, but she did not know why or precisely what steps to take. "If they take me to the hospital," she told Ellen, "don't leave me."

Ellen then went to Alice and Linda's adjoining room and called her brother George at his Long Island law office. By luck she got through. He in turn called their mutual friend, Dr. Kevin Cahill, an expert in tropical disease, reaching him at his Manhattan office. They talked to him together. Meanwhile, the clinic doctor and nurse waited awkwardly in Mary Lee's room. Dr. Cahill suggested that Ellen dismiss the clinic doctor and get in touch with some Maryknoll missionaries he knew in Dar es Salaam. He also said Mary Lee should stop the malaria pills and all other medication, except for Tylenol. If her condition continued to deteriorate, they should try to get her to Nairobi.

While these decisions were being made, the clinic doctor and nurse—who, it should be said in fairness, were perfectly correct from their standpoint in recommending that Mary Lee go to the hospital—waited patiently. Ellen then thanked them and paid them for their time, explaining that the women had decided they would wait until morning before deciding on the hospital. As soon as they left, she called the Maryknoll missionaries, reaching Sister Jean Pruitt, an American nun from California. Although not herself a doctor, Sister Jean said she would get an associate, Dr. Martha Collins, and they would be there shortly. In less than an hour they arrived, accompanied by a black man because, as they explained, they never went out at night without a male escort.

Those who have traveled in distant lands and faced difficulty, frustration, and even danger, know the exquisite relief of finding assistance from one's own countrymen. They speak the same language and idiom, and it is easy to convey the subtleties required for refined communication of medical facts. They understand one's moods, fears, and expectations. So it was with the arrival of these Maryknoll angels of mercy.

Dr. Collins examined Mary Lee's blisters, listened to her heart, and took her temperature. She rubbed her hands slowly over the bones of her legs to determine, it was later learned, if the infection had penetrated the bone marrow, a condition that could quickly be fatal. Meanwhile, she and Sister Jean chatted cheerfully, their calm assurance easing the atmosphere of crisis. Sister Jean suggested that they try to get salt from the hotel to add to the cold compresses which, as recommended by Dr. Cahill, were being placed on the patient's forehead. The women had earlier asked the hotel for salt but had been told none was available. Sister Jean, in undoubtedly authoritative Swahili, obtained it quickly.

The balm of the missionaries' presence brought immediate relief, and Mary Lee felt better and was sure her fever was subsiding. As they watched her, Dr. Collins leafed from time to time through a large medical book open on her lap.

122

Ice wrapped in towels cooled Mary Lee's head; wet towels were also put under her arms. An hour and a half passed; Dr. Collins asked Ellen if she could reach Dr. Cahill again. Ellen went into Alice's room and again, after several insistent attempts, was able to get through. The two doctors discussed the situation and concluded that Mary Lee must be having an allergic reaction, and that it was quite improbable, given the short time in Africa, that she had contracted a disease. Earlier the women had discussed the prospects of getting to a hospital in Nairobi, or even in Europe, but both trips were difficult to work out quickly and travel in Mary Lee's condition would have its own risks. The doctors concluded that if the fever could be brought under control, it would be best to make the short flight inland to the higher elevation and milder climate of Arusha, the heat of the coast now undoubtedly contributing to the spreading infection of the sores. Dr. Collins said that Mary Lee probably had a mild form of Stephen Johnson's syndrome, perhaps compounded by a viral infection. The women asked, "Who was Stephen Johnson?" but got no answer. Weeks later, Ellen learned he was the first person to die of this affliction. Dr. Cahill gave Ellen the names of contacts in Nairobi, in the event that it became necessary to go there, and explained where she could reach him during the next several days. Sister Jean and Dr. Collins also gave Ellen the names of other missionaries to contact in Arusha.

It was near 2:00 A.M. when the visitors left, their stay having wonderfully lifted Mary Lee's morale and confidence. She slept fitfully during the night, Ellen supplying her with wet towels. By morning her fever was lower and they decided to move her to Arusha.

A cab took them to the hot and crowded airport. In a wheelchair, they got Mary Lee to the plane. Late in the afternoon on Friday, December 30, they arrived at the Hotel

77, a cluster of single story cinderblock buildings surrounded by fields of windblown grass, on the outskirts of Arusha. The weather was mild and pleasant, the humidity low, and conditions for resting far better than on the coast. Mary Lee continued to consume large amounts of ginger ale, the only potable liquid she could drink. Ellen called Sister Consulata of the Maryknoll Missionaries of Mary, and she and another nun, Sister Genevieve, a medical doctor, came to the room that evening. They examined the patient, and with what little medicine they had treated the multiple infections that now appeared everywhere on her body.

On Saturday Mr. Lilla and a woman companion from the Tourist Office came to the hotel. He stood awkwardly in the room, smiling and saying he was sorry Mary Lee was sick. The women upbraided him for sending them to Zanzibar when he must have known how bad the "resort" hotel was. He confessed his ignorance. But the women were unassuaged, saying that Americans who spent thousands of dollars to come to Tanzania expected more informed treatment. They would tell others not to come and expose themselves to the difficulties they had experienced. Mr. Lilla could only smile helplessly against the verbal assault.

The sores spread to Mary Lee's eyelids, into her mouth and ears, and down her throat. She could not cry because the tears stung; she worried that her throat would become too inflamed to swallow. Quietly, she prayed.

Chapter 12
Tragedy

Sensing movement and light, I awakened and saw Effatta holding a lantern. He was shaking Tom Jr. Others were stirring too. I pulled out of my sleeping bag and pressed my pocket light. It was 1:10 and cold, but not the sapping cold we had expected. I was warmly dressed and comfortable, but since we were expecting zero temperatures and wind at the top, I stripped to put on long underwear, corduroy pants, and then rain pants. I wore a tee shirt, cotton shirt, sweater, and down jacket. Gloves and mittens, a heavy scarf, and two wool hats, one of which pulled down over most of my face, completed the covering. In my pocket I had a chamois face mask and goggles. My boots were caked with protective wax and the tops covered by gaiters, which enclosed the bottom of my rain pants.

Felix brought tea, biscuits, and marmalade, which we ate by a lantern on the table. The dim light was comforting. Effatta handed each of us an orange and two biscuits "for the summit." We readied our packs for pick-up later by the porters. It was a reassuring exercise, a reminder that the climb had a definite and not-too-distant conclusion.

We were tense and animated. The night had not been as uncomfortable as expected, and most of us had actually slept. No one seemed to be suffering from the predicted headache. Stu had waves of nausea but remained his chipper self.

The only guidebook to Kilimanjaro, which is published by the Mountain Club of Kenya, states that:

Parties usually leave Kibo Hut very early in the morning (by 3:00 A.M.) for the following reasons: (a) to get the benefit of frozen scree; (b) to get a good view of the sun rising behind Mawenzei from high up; (c) because it is quite a good thing not to be able to see the stretch of scree ahead of one, and (d) because one probably cannot sleep in any case [p. 240].

Our situation seemed better. We had been able to sleep and were ready to go. We were not concerned about the scree because it was deep beneath the snow. The odds looked good.

We joked with the other Americans about the stories we would tell, and the embroidery that would be added in later years. In these unrecapturable moments the older among us enjoyed such prospects beyond the comprehension of youth, which takes life's great experiences casually, assuming there will be more, while age has learned that they are indeed limited. Standing in the semi-darkness, I knew we were starting on one of life's unforgettable days.

At 1:45 Effatta said we should leave. We filed out into the night, started at last on the challenge in which so much planning, effort, and expense had been invested. Lining up in single file, we counted to be sure all were present. I checked my pockets, which were stuffed with the emergency blanket, matches, flashlight, compass, sun lotion, the orange and biscuits, and my small camera. My canteen was hooked on my belt. Each of us had his stick. Effatta was in front, I was second, and at the end of the line were Fred and Felix. "Hallelujah," said Effatta, and we moved forward.

We headed northwest on a moderate grade over snow that was dry and firm. Effatta had his flashlight on but the night was clear, without wind, and stars lighted the sky. It was easy to see, and I made out the outline of the mountain and saw flashlights far above. There was comfort in knowing that we were not alone. The pace was steady and I concentrated on Effatta's steps in front of me, only occasionally raising my head to cast an upward glance. My stick went easily through the crust and my boots did not slip. The only sound was the crunch of the snow. No one spoke except for an affirmative grunt when, from time to time, Effatta turned to ask, "Okay?"

We moved upward behind one another, tacking as Effatta thought best. Because of the slow pace, we were able to move steadily for an hour without resting. Stu vomited several times but plugged on. I felt almost normal and avoided abrupt moves, which I knew would start my head pounding.

As the steepness increased, Roland, who was toward the back of the line, began to slip. Fred and Felix called to Effatta, who went back to find out the trouble. Roland's boots did not have the right tread, so Effatta told one of them to move him to a line of exposed scree on the right, across which we were tacking. Thus he managed to continue.

Pressing on, I looked up and in the dark saw two men escorting a third down. Someone muttered that the man was sick. As they passed me I saw that he was Japanese and that the other two, each holding one of his arms, were guides. How disappointing to have to quit at this stage. I knew I would not feel so bad now if it happened to me.

We began to rest more frequently but the time passed quickly and about 4:30 we reached the Cave, a jutting rock halfway to the top, and a natural resting place. It is like a large lean-to, the top high enough for one to stand at the front and to sit comfortably farther back. There was space for all. Effatta, Fred, and Felix lighted their cigarette stubs, as they did at every stop, and sat against the back wall bundled against the cold. Icicles hung from the rock walls around them. The rest of us drank water and breathed deeply, conserving oxygen and energy.

"Doing well, will make it, no worry," Effatta assured us.

Stu stood outside having dry heaves, but the rest of us were in reasonable condition. Tom G. took two pictures with his flash. No one was expecting either, and they catch both our weariness and our determination. There are few pictures anywhere that can equal these for color and drama—the dark rock, the icicles, the pallid faces, the dark outside the Cave, the steep snow-covered slope. As we rested quietly, I was, finally, confident that most and maybe all of us—myself included—would reach the top.

When we got up to leave, the other Americans approached and I heard one exclaim with relief, "Oh, great, here's the Cave." There were now only four of them, the younger girl and her mother having been taken down. Even then this struck me as good judgment. I had seen in the hut that the girl was doing as well or better than the rest of us and I had no doubt that she was in excellent condition. But she and her mother had the good sense not to have to prove anything. One of the men had crampons; his were the only ones I saw on the entire climb. As they settled down to rest in the Cave, we reformed our line outside and to the right. Effatta took his lead position, with me next. At his request, I looked back and asked if everyone was ready. Each called "yes," in order: John, Tom G., Tom, Tom Jr., Stu, Peter, and Roland. Fred and Felix were at the rear. It was 4:55 and we started up.

The moon was high. It was hard to accept that we were only halfway because the summit, although nearly straight up from where we stood, did not look far, and I could see its outline clearly. The stars were extraordinary and I wondered whether the thinner atmosphere might account for their brilliance. Above us there were flashlights below an embankment, and one or two lights above the rim of the embankment. It was astonishing that anyone could be that

Hans Meyer Cave: Peter, John, Tom, and the author

Fred and Effatta at the Hans Meyer Cave

far above us, but I did not have the energy to ponder how they had gotten there. I was close behind Effatta, stepping into his tracks. The grade increased markedly and I began to rely heavily on my stick to avoid slipping. One foot or the other slid a little, tilting me, and several times I felt John steady me with a hand under my elbow. Still, the footing was about what might be expected climbing on snow. As it got steeper, I adjusted by turning to the left and digging in with the right side of my boots. With the stick in my left hand on the downhill side, I was in good balance. Then, as I straightened up a moment to relax, my left foot slipped.

I fell on my back and started to slide rapidly. In quick succession I felt myself brushing against several sticks and boots. I tried to turn to my left to jam my stick into the snow and at the same instant I felt someone grabbing at my leg. But I was not stopping. Then, with a jolt, a hard arm and shoulder jarred me to a stop. Peter had dove on me with a force that left nothing to chance. It took a few moments before we recovered our breath. Then he muttered in my ear, "Will you watch what you're doing." I got up, careful to keep my footing, and assured him and the others I was unhurt. Effatta had come back, concerned about the oldest, and, it appeared, the clumsiest of his charges. He and I then climbed back to the top of the line.

Perhaps it was our unexpectedly good condition, or because we felt secure close together, or because in the dark we were not looking back, or because the summit, now within reach, was beginning to dominate our thoughts; for whatever reason, the fall did not alarm me, or the others. Effatta had come back for fear I had been hurt, but a slip in the snow seemed no more significant than a pre-Freudian slip of the tongue. I have often fallen much harder skiing. True, I was surprised that I had slid so fast, and I would have been even more surprised had I known how far Peter was below me. In a matter of seconds I had whisked past several people, all of whom are quick, agile athletes. In the dark and confusion, none of this registered. Tom Jr. was the one who had grabbed at my leg, but it was Peter, behind him, who stopped me. If he had hesitated for an instant to commit himself, I now doubt that I would have been saved. For although I was attempting to turn and jab in my stick, my acceleration might well have pulled me from it. None of this was then apparent. It was only weeks later, safely at home, watching Peter play hockey, that I realized how his instinct and agility had mastered the moment of crisis and saved my life.

With what now seems incredible unconcern, we continued on, kicking footholds in the crust. There was a tinkling sound on the left and a flashlight, its beam on, went bouncing down the hill. Its speed did not seem threatening, although later I learned that others did not share that view. Then John called up that Tom had lost his stick. It had slipped from his hand and dropped away down the slope. This was an ominous development, but it seemed nothing could be done, and so we continued. Later, Tom Jr. told me, "Dad, of course, said he could do much better without it because you tend to rely on it too much."

We came unexpectedly upon the Japanese, from one of which the flashlight must have escaped. They were bunched up, facing partly downhill; I could not understand why they were headed across our path, moving to our right and descending. Directly above us was the embankment, which was too steep to try head-on. I thought they might have attempted to get around it on the left and, giving that up, were now moving over to try on the other side. We paused while Effatta spoke to their guides. None of us understood what was said. Stopped there in the dark, I didn't hear anyone talk to the Japanese who, we already knew, spoke little if any English. Then they edged across in front of us and disappeared in the dark. Stu told me later that he heard one of their guides say, "Very dangerous," and that he, Stu, had repeated the warning to Effatta. I heard none of this but did hear Effatta, who turned toward us, say, "No problem." He then began to move at an upward slant aiming toward the left side of the embankment.

We soon were beyond the farthest point reached by the Japanese and on snow unmarked by other footholds. I was uneasy, as our line began to stretch out on the side of the slope and we were no longer behind one another. This seemed especially dangerous for Tom, without his stick. But we had confidence in Effatta.

This side of the mountain faces directly east—we must have been approaching 18,000 feet, and were far above anything else in sight. An orange haze was starting to spread across the horizon behind Mawenzi. Although the sun was not yet visible, it was getting light. We now made an upward pointing line and were at varying distances from one another, each having his own difficulty gouging footholds in the snow. The thermometer on my jacket showed 20 degrees Fahrenheit. It was clear and pleasant, without wind. In the increasing light I could see the lip of the summit, still a considerable distance above the embankment. It seemed in reach despite someone saying, "It's still an hour and a half to the top." We were going to do it. The night was behind us and we were at the start of a bright new day. I felt strong and confident.

Then I saw Effatta slip. He was about twenty feet ahead of me and somewhat higher. He had briefly paused, and perhaps straightened up, when one foot went out. He fell and began to slide with startling acceleration down the slope. "Your stick, use your stick," I yelled, but he was sliding in a half-sitting position; in an instant he seemed to leap away from his stick, which catapulted to the side. Helpless and with a growing sense of dread, I watched him cascade down the slope. In a few moments it was clear that he could not stop but was sliding and bouncing faster by the second and that a major disaster was unfolding before us. "No, no, no," I yelled as I saw him fly out over a rock outcropping several hundred feet below, hurtle even faster down the slope, fly out over another rock outcropping, and disappear from view.

John, next behind me, was watching his own feet when he heard me yell. As he looked up, Effatta was sitting on the snow. He kicked in his heels and with both hands tried to drive his stick between his legs. But the stick was pulled back as he held it and shot out from his hands. Until then Effatta looked in control but with the loss of his stick and his alarming acceleration, he was soon spinning helplessly on his back, his arms and legs whirling. John heard me yelling again, "No, no, no," and saw Effatta go out over the first ledge, plunge on, go over the other ledge, and drop from sight.

Tom G. and Tom were near one another, lower and farther back. Each was intent on his own foothold when they heard a yell. When Tom G. looked up, Effatta had already lost his stick and was tilted backward by the force of his fall, his head still up and his hands thrust out for balance. For an instant he looked directly into Tom G.'s eyes, and almost simultaneously, into Tom's, as if to cast a visual lifeline when all else had failed. Both saw in his look the awareness of doom and watched in horror as he plunged down the slope and out over the first ledge, after which, from their positions, he was lost to view.

The others, still farther back and lower, heard my yell but could not immediately tell what had happened. Tom Jr.

saw a man falling, but he seemed to come from above our group. "Who was it?" he called.

Someone answered, "Effatta."

Tom Jr. was incredulous. "Effatta!"

By the time Peter saw him, Effatta was facing downhill, feet and arms thrust out in a braking effort. But the force of his slide threw him on his back and he began to spin and tumble, arms and feet windmilling in the air.

Effatta did not make a sound. After a few terrible moments, he was far below and out sight. All was quiet.

Our group was motionless, the danger now apparent. But reactions varied. John jammed his stick in the snow. "Damn it, damn it," he said, "we were so near the top."

"Calm down," I said heatedly, and I called to Peter, "Can you yell down and see if he is all right?"

But Effatta had fallen hundreds of feet below and was far out of voice range even if we had known where he was and even if there had been someone below to help. John looked up in alarm. I was saying, "We've got to go back to help him," and John thought I was not paying attention to my own hold and might fall too.

In these first uncertain moments he felt a surge of determination to get down safely to see his mother and girlfriend again. He ordered me not to stand upright, to dig my feet in, to push my stick into the snow, and to "Pay attention!"

I have little recollection of his warning and had no sense of being careless. But my preoccupation with Effatta must also have alarmed Stu. His first reaction, which he felt with a sense of guilt, was relief; now he could stop with honor. Looking at me he called up, "Forget it, Andy. He's dead. Let's get ourselves down."

But I couldn't shake the thought that Effatta was lying somewhere below, smashed up and suffering, if not dead, and there was nothing we could do, no one to call to, no way to help if help in time might save his life, only the vast slope and the silence below.

The Japanese must have seen Effatta as he fell. I could make them out, far below and to our left, their line motionless. Still farther down were the four Americans. They had also stopped; everyone was considering his precarious stance. Tom Jr. kept asking himself how we had gotten into such a spot.

"No one move; dig your feet in and use your stick until we figure this out," I yelled down the line in another superfluous directive. "We will have to go back the way we came, but dig in, one step at a time. Don't move one foot until the other's in place, and brace with your stick. Don't rely on a single foot; make sure that one foot and your stick are in place before the other foot moves."

I was scarcely aware that I was repeating a rule often followed on family climbs. From the first time we had gone up the headwall of Tuckerman's Ravine on Mount Washington, I had impressed on the children the necessity on steep climbs, where hands and feet were required, of never, never, never relying on one foot but always to have a handhold, and if possible two, that will save you if your in-place foot slips or your foothold gives way as you step up. This simple, vital maxim equally applied now, when our sticks were our surrogate handholds. I should have drilled the rule home sooner on this climb—and would have, if we had foreseen the danger from the snow. If Effatta had followed the rule, he would not have fallen.

The sunlight was now on the snow, exposing the crust in all its treacherous glitter. Getting down was a terrifying prospect because we were suddenly aware that a single slip was fatal. How best to proceed provoked a grimly humorous debate. Tom, without a stick, calmly explained to Tom

G. that it was best to keep all one's weight on one's feet and press them into the snow. This, it is true, is a first principle for rock climbing. But Tom G. and Tom Jr. disagreed on its applicability here, urging that it was safer to crouch down, pressing the stick or hand into the slope even if that took some vertical weight off the feet. For a few painful minutes this discussion went on in classroom tones, each of them citing "rules" as to centers of gravity, the comparative values of vertical weight and horizontal force-holds, and other "principles of physics." Tom Jr. burst out in dismay, "Come on, Dad, this is serious," but Tom held to his view.

With a caution that was overwhelming, compared to our insouciant ascent, we began to edge across the slope. Those who have climbed mountains know that getting down, although less rigorous, can be far more dangerous than climbing up. The footholds we'd kicked in on our ascent, when our weight was pressed forward into the mountain, were too shallow for the descent. They were also in a direction and at an angle opposite to what was required for a toehold coming down. Reaching a foot down, and shifting weight to kick in a foothold, was tricky business. Those below had the initial problem, but following them was of little benefit. I found I could not use their footholds because the bottom part of the snow had often been pulled away when they withdrew their feet.

Without a stick Tom continued to be at the greatest risk. Tom G. passed down his stick, and Tom used it for one or two steps, then handed it back. By this expedient, they managed, in alternating moves, to proceed over and downward. After several exchanges, Tom reached an icy stretch. He had to slide a short distance but went farther than he intended, too far to hand back the stick. Tom G. was stranded. His toes were dug in, and he leaned into the hill, pushing his fists into the snow. He looked back at John and said, "I think I'm going to panic."

"No, you're not," John said. "You can do it. You *have* to!"

The lack of an alternative eliminates panic. Tom G. pulled his arms out, and turned halfway to the right. Then, he stepped forward and slid to where Tom could grab him.

John used a different technique. He was facing uphill, and proceeding backwards, as on a ladder. With one foot in place, and his left hand holding his stick on the downhill side, he used the other foot to kick a purchase in the snow; getting that foot in place, he moved his stick lower. Then he pulled the upper foot down and with it kicked a new foothold. *This is taking forever,* he thought, *but it makes no difference. I am going to get down safely.*

Tom Jr. was in the same stance but was stopped above an icy patch. Peter told him to turn but Tom Jr. thought he would lose his balance, the awful expanse of open slope staring up at him. He managed to turn, his weight precariously balanced between the vertical and horizontal, and slide across, jamming his stick in at the first spot of snow beyond and bringing himself to a precarious halt. He closed his eyes with relief.

I could not force myself to turn around and back down the hill. Instead, I kicked in from the side, with my stick planted below me, and kept virtually all my weight on my feet. In retrospect, John's method seems safer, but at the time I feared that my feet would slip out and I would slide away on my stomach. In the danger of those moments individual instincts prevailed, as they should, over theory and advice, however well intended. Each of us was built differently, our weights varied, and we used our arms and legs differently for balance and safety. Each of us had to decide his own right way. We could not, we starkly knew, make a single mistake or relax for an instant our tense control. There was no margin for error. We instinctively applied the DeGaullian precept, "Take no advice but your own."

The sun moved higher, the heat and glare increasing. Our objective, as we looked below, was to cross over to the tracks of the Japanese. Those in the front of their line appeared to be chopping footholds with ice axes. This explained their clumping up on the hill. It was an hour before we reached their tracks. Then we worked our way down, coming up behind them. The other Americans were there too. It was a strange assemblage: several Japanese in front chopping in the snow and behind them, seeking safety in their tracks, fifteen more Japanese, twelve Americans, and six or eight guides.

As we moved lower, we searched for signs of Effatta, but saw nothing. Then one of the Americans called up that a guide at the front of the Japanese group reported that someone with a broken leg was below on a rock. Several called, hopefully, "Where, where?" Someone asked, "Could he have survived?" But there was no further word. Nor could we see anything! As the minutes passed, hope dwindled.

Then I saw the outcropping that formed the top of the Cave; it was about three hundred feet below me. Studying the slope to the left, I saw a small, sentrylike figure on a rock rising out of the snow. There was something in front of him and with awful certainty I knew it was Effatta. We were still too far to call down. But Felix, behind me, must have heard someone call in Swahili. He touched my shoulder and said, "They say dead."

"Are you certain, is that correct?" I asked, still wanting to hope, but he nodded.

I saw Fred crying. He said to Stu, "Effatta, he finished."

Effatta lay some fifty yards across from the Cave, in a dip in the slope, just before it again falls off sharply. The area looked like a primeval graveyard, with slabs of rock sticking up from the snow. These had stopped his slide but only by smashing him to death. Fred and Felix made their way down to the body and one of them reached into Effatta's jacket and took out some paper. With three other guides from the Japanese group helping, they dragged the body across to the Cave. They slipped frequently, and, once clear of the rocks, had difficulty keeping themselves and the body from sliding farther down the slope.

When they reached the Cave, they left the body at the entrance, removed Effatta's orange wind jacket, and pulled his blue jacket up to cover his head. Globs of blood on the outside indicated the battering beneath. Other guides and most of the Japanese were standing at the Cave when we arrived. Fred said they would need a stretcher and helpers from the Kibo Hut to get the body down. There were tears on Stu's cheeks, marking the bigness of heart that is his finest quality. He embraced and shook hands with Fred and Felix; following his lead, the rest of us did the same. Only a few words were spoken across the barriers of language and emotion. The Japanese and the other guides stood by somberly.

The place and circumstances, however, precluded indulging in grief or reflection. We were below the most dangerous part but were still high and had a long and precarious slope to get down. Everyone knew that he could not allow himself to be distracted, even by death, from concentrating on the immediate task of descending safely. The Japanese started down, those with ice axes chopping the way. We followed behind. I looked toward the top and saw two figures, which I took to be the climbers whose lights I had seen in the night. They must have made Gillman's Point and were now descending. One of them, rugged looking and probably in his late twenties, passed on my left, moving down rapidly. He held to a crouched position, his right hand grasping a steel spike, ready to stab it into the snow. It was obvious from this single implement that he was not a novice. Probably he knew nothing of our tragedy and never looked toward us; soon he was far below. I did not see his companion go by.

In the daylight I could now see that the Cave was at the top of a rock rampart, perhaps 1,000 feet high, which the ancient volcano had thrown across the face of the mountain and which separated the snowy area above from a similar slope below. The rampart itself was impassable, but the route we had taken up in the dark, and were now to retrace, moved out on the south side and then down through a wide valley of snow that provided a pass through the wall of rock. Still following the Japanese, who had been trading off the ice axes as one after another became exhausted, we proceeded down this passage to the top of the broad open slope beneath the rampart. There it was not so steep or slippery and in places there was exposed scree. Here the Japanese choppers had paused to rest. We shook hands with them, repeating to each, *"Arigato, toxon arigato,"* "Thank you, thank you very much." None of those I saw spoke English but they understood our gratitude, replying to me, *"Doi toshi mashte,"* "You are welcome." From here down it appeared that, if care was taken, there was sufficient breakage in the snow and exposed scree to make the footing safe. Nevertheless, we paid close attention because even here, if one stepped away from the path that was being broken, there was nothing to prevent falling another thousand feet. The glare was now intense and the temperature was rising rapidly. I was soaked beneath my heavy clothing and two ski hats, but took nothing off for fear that trying to do so might momentarily restrict my mobility and cause me to slip. I knew also that much of the perspiration was the healthy product of the concentration on getting down safely.

The Kibo Hut is the only man-made object from the summit to the Horombo Huts miles below. Standing at the Kibo Hut, one can look over two miles up the mountain to Gillman's Point and the eastern summit rim. The top seems in reach—neither too high nor too far. Coming down, the perspective is entirely different. The hut, which I could not see until we were well below the Cave, appears no larger than the top of a tin can in the panorama below. When we finally arrived, our porters and others from the Japanese group were standing around the cooking hut. Livingstone was there. One of the Africans, a man who seemed to be the caretaker, came up to me, nodded at Livingstone and said, "He, Effatta's son."

I was astonished. Yet the words had a ring of truth. Livingstone was the one who had brought me Effatta's notebook and pictures. It was Livingstone I had seen running off after a sharp order from Effatta. I put my arms around Livingstone and held him, conscious of the anguish beneath his expressionless face.

It was 9:30. We went in to our bunks to wait while the guides started up with a stretcher. The Japanese were in the large room on the left. Looking down the stone hallway, I saw two Africans holding a stretcher upright and inserting straps to hold a body in place. The stretcher had a bicycle-type wheel underneath for rolling it on the trail. Felix surprised us with biscuits and tea. Although no one had thought of food, we had been on the move for almost eight hours and, except for tea and a biscuit at 1:00 A.M., had had no food and almost no liquid for sixteen hours. In fact, we had had nothing substantial since breakfast the day before.

Tom and Peter near the bottom of the summit cone

I had even forgotten to drink water since we rested at the Cave on the ascent, and now noticed that my plastic canteen was bent in and contained a solid block of ice. The steady night climb, the trauma of Effatta's fall, and the tenseness of the descent had so stimulated our systems that food seemed unnecessary, and none of us felt either hungry or tired. There was relief at being safe and at knowing it would be easy hiking down, but the day's events were not finished and we were not yet relaxed.

We stretched on our bunks. The other Americans were there, but no one felt like talking and they soon left for Horombo. Sometime later Fred came in and signalled for Tom to come outside. The rest of us followed as Fred walked to the guides' hut. There we saw that no one had yet started back up the mountain, and that an argument was underway as to who would retrieve the body. The man I took for the caretaker shook his head when I asked about the delay. "No stretchers; two stretchers used for sick men gone." He had, he indicated, sent word to Horombo for a stretcher to be brought up. Since the round trip was twelve to fourteen miles, it was obvious that there would be no chance that day to get the body. Furthermore, Felix would not go back up to help bring down the body. When I questioned him, he pointed to his knee, saying, "Hurt."

Fred pointed at Felix's head, "It there, not his knee."

For a few minutes we stood in stalemate. Then Felix changed his mind. One of the other guides took off his boots and gave them to Felix, who put them on and said, "Ready."

It was 11:00. I told Fred, who had clearly taken charge, that the rest of us would start for Horombo and wait for him there. I said I would carry my pack, not feeling I could ask Livingstone. Then I learned that Fred, the moment we had gotten back to Kibo, had sent Jasper, John's porter, to

144

the Gate to tell them of the accident. Since some of the porters would also be needed to carry the body, most of us decided to carry our packs. Fred protested, a credit to his sense of duty, but we insisted and left only one pack and two sleeping bags for the porters.

The younger four set out immediately, followed by Tom G. and me. Tom and Stu were last, alternating in carrying Stu's pack. Both appeared tired and moved slowly. I continued to be surprised that I felt strong, despite my heavy pack and the even heavier burden of the thoughts that weighed upon us. The grim reality of death, the small, preventable slip, the terrible, irretrievable loss to Effatta's wife and children, all were thoughts that cast a gloom upon us even as, slowly descending, we breathed easier with every step and the warm sun was, so far as it could be, comforting, if not cheering. Tom and Stu fell behind. As we moved onto the Saddle they soon became smaller and then disappeared from view.

Tom G. and I talked little, each with his own thoughts. It was undeniable that Effatta had been guilty of a major misjudgment, and had exposed all of us to the possibility of meeting his own grisly fate. Many of us, especially Tom, who lacked a stick, and Roland, whose boots lacked the right tread, might have been killed; indeed, I was certain that if Effatta's fall had not caused us to stop, one or more of us would have been killed. With our lack of crampons and ice axes, it was not possible for eight of us to have succeeded in crossing that deadly slope. It was also hard to believe that so many climbers, that same night, were on the mountain and exposed to the same danger. This must have been true on preceding nights as well! For we had heard of the rain and snow from four different groups at the Kibo Hotel, as well as from the climbers we had seen on the way up.

We were expecting bad weather and knew we might be turned back by wind or snow, or stopped by ice. We had been prepared, we thought, for every contingency. No one, with one exception, had mentioned any danger from slipping—all the emphasis had been placed on the lack of oxygen, fatigue, the wet and cold. And the brief warning about slipping had not impressed us. I spent some time wondering why. There seemed to be two reasons: first, the impression we had of the speaker, and second, the circumstances in which his warning occurred.

The missionary's hearty approach had generated warm feelings but had not suggested that he knew much about the mountain. He did not appear an experienced climber; his daughters seemed to look out for him as he moved good-naturedly up the mountain. I had been surprised when the three left Horombo at noon on the third day, as soon as the rain stopped, and headed for the Kibo Hut. I was more surprised to meet him returning on the Saddle, descending while we were still climbing, and to learn that he had made the summit. His caution about having "two sticks for coming down," and his remark that "one fellow slid and went whoosh but was saved when he stopped on a ledge," were perfectly explicit but somehow lacked the tone of serious danger, suggesting instead minor risks of the kind a hiker might expect.

Another reason for my failure to appreciate his warning was that danger from slipping was not in our well-prepared catalogue of concerns. A person is hindered as well as helped by experience. Experience had drilled us to be prepared for contingencies; through reading and discussion, I thought we had identified all the serious obstacles to the climb. Alert to the known obstacles, we were close-minded to new ones. We were overdependent on our preparation, confident that there were no serious unexpected dangers ahead. Thus mentally relaxed, our energy was concentrated on known obstacles—lack of oxygen, the cold, the steepness of the final push.

Accustomed to a world where dangers are nearly always well-defined—"construction ahead," "bridge freezes before road surface"—it is hard to appreciate that real danger may lie ahead but no one will give a warning. This was more the case because the large number of climbers we had seen from the start—and were still seeing on the Saddle—made the experience far from a solitary effort. There was great comradeship and a feeling of solidarity all the way, without the least impression of unexpected dangers.

And, of course, we had put too much reliance on Effatta and his assistants. They were so at ease on the mountain. It was not only their bearing and the respect the others accorded Effatta; it was also the fact that the packs and food seemed to move so easily up the mountain day after day, rain or shine. Most of all, it was the confidence instilled by the meals, well cooked and delicious, served on time at dawn and dusk under circumstances that anywhere else in the world would be considered impossible. Four days of such treatment, and one unconsciously stuffs one's judgment in the bottom of one's pack and stops thinking for oneself.

Our group was stretched out over the Saddle when we met the missionary on the way up, the younger hikers in front. I was not sure who else heard his warning, and I wondered whether, if it had reached younger and more expedient dispositions, it would have taken hold. Later I learned that several of the others had heard it, but to little effect. And what could we have done about falling rocks? You couldn't see them, much less hear them at night.

Except for the missionary, no one had mentioned this as a problem.

In fact, as it turned out, we encountered no such problem. We had seen one flashlight fall down the slope, and I had seen one rock roll down slowly. Neither was going fast enough to injure anyone and the odds of being hit were negligible, considering the expanse of the slope. As for the snow, we would have been more careful, perhaps, but what else? The missionary had not suggested one might slip climbing *up*; his warning was about coming down. Who would suppose that even on a steep slope—and steep as it was the slope did not require crawling up—a single slip would launch one like a human toboggan to be smashed to death below?

This did not square with my experience on ski slopes, where I had slipped many times, but never far or fast enough to be killed. Who ever heard of a skier who, from a standstill position, slid to his death? I had seen *The Man Who Skied Down Everest.* There the skier trailed two parachutes, but was nevertheless going over one hundred miles an hour when he fell. Although he slid a considerable distance in the snow, with the deflated parachutes providing scant drag, he came to a stop short of a precipice. It seemed to me this was the usual outcome for a fallen skier. Even now it is hard to comprehend the difference between even the biggest ski slope and the enormous snow-covered cone of Kilimanjaro.

Another factor was that the warning came on the Saddle—an elevated desert and a different world from the arctic summit route. The challenge of the Saddle is to move slowly to avoid wearing out. We had not yet reached the snow when the missionary passed us. Getting to Kibo Hut was that day's project, and we did not have the extra energy to worry about slipping on snow later.

For these reasons, the missionary's crucial words went virtually unheeded. When no one else we saw mentioned danger and we saw no one hurt at the Kibo Hut, I forgot his warning.

Apart from the warning, why wasn't the danger apparent as we approached the moment of tragedy? Although no one else had mentioned sliding—and after the missionary, we must have passed fifty people, including the Belgian group, before reaching Kibo Hut—we had two other warnings: the sliding flashlight and my own slip in the snow. The first, even in retrospect, does not seem significant. I felt the light was sliding too slowly to suggest danger. My slip was of a different order. There could have been no more definite clue. Indeed, it was exactly the same as Effatta's slip, and but for Peter might have had the same result. Yet it did not then register on any of us what peril we were in. Nor, apparently, did it register on the guides.

I can explain our incredible misjudgment only by noting our lack of awareness of the size of the slope and the great opportunity it provided for a sliding object to accelerate, without hindrance, for hundreds and hundreds of feet. If we had climbed in daylight we might have realized this, for we had been moving upward four and a half hours. But in the darkness, especially when concentrating on one's physical condition and literally taking one step at a time, it is hard to appreciate how far one has come, how vast a hill stretches below, and where on the slope one is at a particular time.

The subtle change in the condition of the snow as we moved upward was also entirely beyond our thought or knowledge. Yet it was this change, more than any other factor, that accounted for Effatta's fall. I have said that considerable snow had fallen on the upper reaches of the mountain in the days preceding our arrival at the Kibo Hut, but that the weather cleared Thursday morning and the sun shone that day and Friday. More important, the temperature was comparatively warm—in the fifties during the day at the Kibo Hut, and above freezing higher up during part of the day when the sun shone directly on the eastern side of the mountain, on the route we were to take. As a result, the snow immediately above the Kibo Hut was soft under a thin crust that broke beneath one's foot and gave no hint of slipping. Other climbers had left a trail in the snow immediately above the hut, and hikers descending on the previous day had so broken the snow that we were not likely to slip ascending in the same tracks. Farther up, however, the tracks disappeared, and at any rate the immense slope offered no identifiable route. At the higher levels also the snow, warmed by the sun during the day, had been treated to sharply lower temperatures at night. This must have happened between sundown Friday and midnight, soon after which we began the final ascent. The higher we went, the more the nighttime cold had crusted the snow which had been wet from Friday's sun. This imperceptible but ascending increase in the thickness of the crust formed a sliding board that, with the sharp upward grade above the Cave, became increasingly dangerous the higher we went.

Effatta's size was a possible factor in the tragedy. He was small and wiry, weighing perhaps 135 pounds. A heavier man might more easily have kicked into the snow. His cane, too, was much less effective than our crude but rugged steeltipped sticks. My impression the instant before he fell is that he was holding the cane loose and above the snow; he must have relaxed just a moment when his foot slipped. His orange outer parka was nylon, and it slid easily on the snow. This deadly combination—crust, grade, weight, cane, parka—all contributed to the speed of his fall.

No one was near enough to help him once he slipped, but I still cannot accept that all was from that instant lost. Losing his cane—which happened so soon after he fell—deprived him of his best means of stopping. I wondered if he could have recovered it to slow himself if it had been strapped to his wrist. None of us had taken that precaution. None of the sticks carried straps, which is why Tom lost his. It is so elementary a precaution when climbing on snow, and was so universally ignored, by us and by every hiker we saw. This alone shows the gap between the dangers we faced and the adequacy of our preparations. I later saw that some of the Japanese carried ski poles with wrist straps, but I believe they did so because they already had them and not to prevent loss in the snow. Except for the summit approach, there was of course no risk of losing a stick and no one gave any thought to the matter.

Without a stick, spike, or ice axe, what could Effatta have done? As soon as he lost his stick, his arms went out in an effort to balance himself and a moment later in an effort to break his fall. This was an instinctive move to protect his head from falling back and being battered. But it was a fatal blunder. By keeping his balance in the first vital moments, he went down the slope sitting up; thus his position contributed to his acceleration by reducing the friction which might have slowed him. Instead of holding himself up, he should have turned on his stomach, kicking and beating furiously into the snow. Whether that would have made a difference, no one can say.

Could he have done anything else? Perhaps try to stand up and run across or even down the hill? Jamming feet into the snow in a wild effort to stand and run, even while sliding, might have impeded the fall. It is easier to ponder such moves than to perform them, especially in the brief period between life and death as one hurtles down a mountain. I have been told by others who survived similar falls that the force of the slide makes it impossible to twist as I am suggesting and that, as acceleration increases, one is helpless. Nonetheless, it is worth considering such possibilities and experimenting on small hills before exposing oneself to the dangers we faced. There is more than a single instant to react to a sudden fall. A falling body in a vacuum, where there is no friction, accelerates at the rate of thirty-two feet per second. This means it is dropping at a speed of thirty-two feet per second after the first second, sixty-four feet per second after the second second, ninety-six feet per second after the third second, and so on. Effatta's rate of fall was far less—I would guess five or six feet per second—so that in the early seconds, at least, there would have been some chance. He had tried to drive his stick in the snow, and the effort, although unsuccessful, must have slowed him a little.

One does not lose one's wits the moment one slips. I know that in the moments after I slipped, I was intent on turning to strike in my stick even as I slid. I had not panicked when Peter stopped me. This was not because I am cool in danger, but because I had no awareness of danger and was absorbed in trying to stop. Nor had Effatta panicked. If I had yelled, "Get up and run," instead of, "Your stick, use your stick," or if we had discussed such a situation in advance, would it have made a difference? Certainly, those who climb in snow should test such possibilities.

These considerations are in some way similar to instructions I read years ago about ocean swimming. People often drown when caught in an undertow which pulls them under and out, even in shallow water. I know of a man who drowned when pulled out by an unusual current while vacationing, of all safe places, on a Caribbean island. Such deaths are preventable if people understand what is happening and do not panic. When caught in such a tow, do not struggle against it. Instead—and one's life depends on knowing this—relax and go out with the undertow. There will be a few terrifying moments—maybe even a minute or more—while being swept out to sea, but shortly the pull subsides and one will float up to the surface. Then it is no great problem to swim back to shore. Struggling initially against the tow causes panic and quick exhaustion, with drowning a real possibility. In a different way, but to the same purpose, if Effatta had tried to run or lunge, downward and partly across the fall-line, he might conceivably have slowed himself and saved his life. Once he had slipped and lost his stick, there was no other choice.

Of course, the practical way to avoid such tragedy is to have crampons and ice axes. We had neither, and it remains incomprehensible to me that climbers are allowed on the snow above Kibo Hut without them. It may be that people would resist lugging this weight up the mountain, especially if the snow had not accumulated when they left the Gate. But the caretaker at the Kibo Hut could keep such equipment and not allow guides to take people higher without it. This is so simple a matter when the difference, as for us, was life or death. The trouble was taken to build a large stone building at 15,500 feet. It would be little additional trouble to keep ice axes and crampons there! Effatta's fellow guides should insist on it, for themselves and for the unsuspecting climbers. In the snow, with crampons and ice axes, roping should also be required. Without crampons and axes, roping is questionable. Effatta might have been saved if we were roped together—or we all might have fallen. It probably would have been a question of whether, at the critical moment, I had a strong foothold. If so, he might not have pulled John and the others down the line, but, lacking crampons and considering our precarious footing, it is better we were not roped.

All these thoughts battled accusingly with one another as we moved across the Saddle. But they provided no relief from reality; they were all too late.

Jasper, on his way to the Gate, must have alerted the caretakers at the Horombo and Mandara Huts. A number of ascending hikers, however, had left Horombo early that day. As we came upon them crossing the Saddle, we asked each if he had heard the news. Most had not. Some spoke English but a few spoke neither English nor French. This created a problem and we made sure, in various ways, that each understood there was real danger on the snow.

Three or four days up from the Gate, most of them having traveled at great expense from Europe or America, uniformly in excellent condition, nearing the object of all their plans and effort, literally at the apex of their Great Adventure, with little hope probably of a second chance, and crossing the trackless Saddle in the warm sun of an unmenacing day, it must have been colossally irritating to be accosted by our tale of warning and woe. Who were these disheveled Americans, carrying their own packs, without guides or porters, claiming the snow was dangerous and could be fatal? Those who understood English and could grasp the full story tried to appreciate our warning, but still they had the overpowering urge to look on Effatta's death as our problem rather than theirs. Their faces could not hide the reluctance with which they forced themselves to listen. They seemed ready to protest that someone else's tragedy ought not to require that they pull up short with the top in sight only a single day away. So, after a few minutes, they moved on, a cloud spreading over their cheerful adventure. Two small groups, one American and the other English, both led by men in their early forties,

154

were more responsive. One said he thought Kibo would be as far as he would go because it "sounds too risky" higher up. Another was less explicit, but I saw he recognized the danger. They were the exceptions—people who looked reality in the face, their judgment unclouded by disappointment.

One hiker, crossing the Saddle alone, spoke only French, a rare person to be found on foreign soil. *"Notre guide a tombé sur la neige,"* I explained in my execrable accent. *"Il est trés dangereau."* He nodded in courteous agreement.

Turning toward the mountain, and with a sweep of my hand to indicate Effatta's slide, I added somberly, *"Il était tué; il est mort."*

His eyes widened and I knew I had made my point. *"Tué?"* he repeated, and I nodded, *"Oui."*

Another pair spoke only German. We tried hard to convey our message but in the end were not sure they understood more than that something had happened and someone was dead. For them I counted on Stu, and later learned he spoke to them.

A young porter was heading up, a bag on his head. After the usual *"Jambo,"* we asked if he had heard of the accident. "Yes, bad news," he replied. We told him Effatta was our guide, whereupon he explained that he was from Effatta's "table," by which we discovered he meant Effatta's family. He added, "I am Effatta's son."

With some hesitation we expressed our sympathy and shook his hand. Then, as we started to move off, he asked if he could borrow our gaiters for the snow. It seemed an odd request and we explained that they belonged to the Kibo Hotel. "No problem," he assured us, "can return to Kibo." It was, of course, possible that he was Effatta's son, and his mournful expression made us, vulnerable as we were, sympathetic. But Tom G. and I politely explained we thought it better if we returned the gaiters ourselves. He quickly dropped the matter and continued on his way. He had a fine sense of proportion, gauging that his credibility was worth no more than a pair of gaiters.

Descending the Saddle is easy, even with packs, and we reached the southeastern border by early afternoon. Then we moved slowly up the small barrier hill and across the area of rocks and brush that turns down to the "Last Water." Here peanuts and water made a satisfying lunch. It is remarkable how fit one feels with exercise and a forced fast. The steady, easy shedding of excess fat supplies energy without fatigue and there is no craving for food because none is available. Nor does one have any other discomfort; there is just the opposite feeling of buoyancy and vigor.

Two Japanese couples had stopped for lunch a little ahead of us. They were neat and well dressed in red jackets and knickers, hardly looking like they had been on the trail for several days. Probably they were from the group we had followed after the accident, but the obstacles of language again prevented conversation. In the warm sun and pastoral setting, the morning seemed a long time ago.

We pushed on, the trail rising and falling and small bushes becoming more abundant. About four o'clock we came around the south side of a hill and saw the Horombo Huts. Smoke rose from the cooking sheds and a scattering of porters and guides sat on the ground outside. Tom G. and I went to the main hut but did not see any of our group. We then located the caretaker. He said our group had one hut and we had the choice of one or two bunks in each of three other huts. He told me climbers had arrived from Mandara as early as 8:00 A.M. to be sure of bunks. The hut with two unoccupied bunks had a sick man in it. I asked

156

whether a stretcher had been taken up to Kibo Hut, but he said there had been no one to take it. Nearby I saw a stretcher, with a center wheel beneath.

Some of our group were at our hut; the hut with the two empty bunks was nearby. I walked over and opened the door. A Japanese, pale as death, was lying in the bunk on the left, his eyes closed. A companion, sitting in another bunk, protested the intrusion. Quickly I backed out, knowing that none of us could sleep in the small A-frame with a man with an unknown illness. It did not occur to me that this might be the climber the guides brought down in the night. Nor did I pause to consider what was wrong with the man in the bunk, other than that he seemed quite ill. We arranged that the older of us—Tom, Stu, and I—should have three bunks, and Tom G. the fourth. He and Tom Jr., however, volunteered to take bunks in other huts so that John, Peter, and Roland could stay with us, two of them in the center on the floor.

Tom and Stu arrived, weary but improving with the lower altitude. Tom's and Roland's sleeping bags and a pack had been left for the porters. We now knew no stretcher had been sent up, and because of the delay in starting up from Kibo for the body, it seemed unlikely that Fred and the others would have started for Horombo and risked being caught by darkness. So, we had no food and Tom and Roland no sleeping bags. I inquired of the caretaker but he said, "No food," although he would try to find some tea and biscuits. True to his word, he brought them to the main hut a little later, and with nuts and raisins from my pack, this made our dinner.

About 6:30, when we were getting ready for bed, a porter came with the surprising news that Fred had arrived with the body. We found him near the caretaker's hut, standing with the others. Fred is of moderate height, with a crouch to his shoulders. This is not, as one might suppose, from hiking or carrying packs, but seems to be a position adapted to maximize his draw on a cigarette, as if life depended on pulling the smoke to the ultimate reaches of his lungs. This he and the others were doing, their casual stance offering no hint of the day's ordeal. A few yards away, in the lonely stillness of death, lay Effatta, wrapped in canvas, on a rustic stretcher.

Tom's and Roland's bags were brought to our hut and Felix came to say our dinner had arrived and would soon be ready. Godfrey had sent the food up that day to meet us, an arrangement that had never occurred to me but was of course the logical and efficient thing to do. Felix spread the tablecloth, put out the silverware, and, already full of snacks, we nevertheless proceeded with a normal meal.

I still had Effatta's notebooks, and was uncomfortably aware that ours would be the final entry. His wife and family were entitled to some special words from us. I had not seen Livingstone since that morning but he was much on my mind. Back in my bunk, with the others bedding down, I wondered what to say. Shining my pocket light on the paper, I leafed through the pages of happy tributes. Then I wrote our own:

December 31, 1983
Today our guide and friend, Effatta, died near the summit of Mt. Kilimanjaro. From the start of our climb from Kibo Hotel on December 27, Effatta had made our climb a wonderful experience. His assistant guides and porters did everything for our comfort—pleasantly and efficiently under Effatta's wise guidance. At 1:00 A.M. today Effatta woke us to begin the final climb to the top from Kibo Hut. All proceeded smoothly and we were well above the Cave when suddenly Effatta slipped on the frozen snow and slid rapidly

down the steep slope and out of sight far below. He did not make a sound.

We admired his skill as a guide and his qualities of leadership, which all the porters and other guides acknowledged. Effatta had the satisfaction of knowing he was the best. And he was a friend to all of us. We extend our deep sympathy to his wife and family and especially to Livingstone who has been with us these past days and who can be proud that he had Effatta as his father and example.

I then passed it around, and each of us signed.

Unexpectedly, several Africans arrived at our hut and I was called outside. The caretaker introduced me to a park ranger who had arrived from the Gate to accompany us down with the body. The ranger said that I would have to stay with the body and that Fred and I would take it to the police station at Moshi, there to give a full report of the accident before the body was taken to the morgue. We were to be ready to leave at 8:00 the next morning. As we got back again into our sleeping bags Stu lightened our spirits by grumbling that "this is the first New Year's Eve I've had to go to bed with five other guys." A moment later he added, "and the last."

Stretched out warm and safe in my bunk—quiet in the dark, without distractions, in those reflective moments before sleep when one is, if ever, completely honest with oneself—the tension and drama receded. There remained the persistent but futile conviction that events might have been different, that the accident should not have happened. In a few seconds, a slip left Effatta dead, and his wife—especially his wife—and children forever deprived. As much as I felt for them, I felt an even greater dread of the responsibility that would have been mine if the body of one of us, rather than Effatta's body, now lay nearby. I was not responsible for him but I was, beyond question,

159

responsible to Mary Lee for John and Peter and myself. To a large extent I was responsible for the others. I thanked God that we had been spared.

Strangely, because all of us must have had similar thoughts, I slept soundly, without dreams, and I believe the others did also. The completeness of the experience—from the tense nighttime start to the accident, followed by the long hike down—must have left us with a sense of the whole, without loose ends. And despite innumerable later reflections I have never had a nightmare about it, although each terrible moment of Effatta's fall is as vivid to me now as when it occurred.

Chapter 13

The Cortege

I awoke at 6:00, as the early light sifted into the hut. We organized our gear for the final day's hike, relieved that the cold and the challenges were over. At breakfast in the main hut we reviewed again what I had written in Effatta's book. Stu said Effatta had taught his climbers a phrase or two of Swahili whenever they talked with him, and so we included that in our small eulogy. Then, feeling the lack of the most important and consoling sentiment, I added at the end, just before the signatures:

Into Thy Hands, O God!

When our packs were ready, I went to fill my canteen near the cooking huts. The body was not in sight; it must have been taken into one of the huts for the night. There had been no indication of animals at this elevation, but it had occurred to me the night before that a corpse might attract whatever was around.

Fred and Felix appeared with a few of the porters. Livingstone and some of the others were missing. Knowing that several porters were needed to carry the body, we said we could take our own packs, but Fred, courteous and definite, made it clear that that was their job, at least for the older members of our group. The younger ones, however, could help. Going down, he noted, was not a great problem, although the loads a few of the porters took were still astonishing.

It was a beautiful morning, and we snapped pictures of each other and of the porters adjusting their loads. Then

161

I thought of the signs I had made for the summit. Before leaving for Africa, I had written on a large sheet the words

HARTZELL ASCENT
MT. KILIMANJARO
1983

and had packed it away, with an American flag, to be used for a picture at the summit. Since weight was to be minimized, I had—craftily, I thought—written on the top of a second sheet the words "Gelwicks Ascent," and upside-down on the bottom of the same sheet "Law Ascent." By holding the top and bottom, respectively, of the second sheet over the top two words of the first, we could get three group pictures with appropriate references to Hartzell, Gelwicks, and Law. I had smiled thinking how those pictures would look in law offices in New York, Cincinnati, and Washington. So I pulled out the first sheet. A Japanese man standing nearby, the friend of the sick man, cheerfully took several pictures. One shows us holding the American flag and the sign

HARTZELL ASCENT
MT. KILIMANJARO
1983

Then, to everyone's surprise, I turned the top of the second sheet over the first line, and another picture was taken with the sign reading

GELWICKS ASCENT
MT. KILIMANJARO
1983

Using the bottom of the second sheet, inverted, we then got

LAW ASCENT
MT. KILIMANJARO
1983

It was, briefly, a happy scene.

We moved out to the front of the main hut, and the younger four headed down. Frank would be waiting at the Gate at 1:30. I knew they could come close to being on time, and found out later that they had covered the distance in a little over four hours, no minor feat when carrying heavy packs from that altitude and over those trails.

I then looked over and saw Effatta's body, which had been brought out from one of the porter's huts. Other Africans were bringing up the wheel-stretcher and I heard someone say it was for the sick Japanese. These preparations for the march to the bottom and civilization created a strange impression, as if we were part of some ancient caravan. I did not see the sick Japanese being brought out but, when I looked a few minutes later, the Africans were strapping him on the stretcher; he had a sickly color and seemed barely conscious, although his head moved a little from time to time.

Stu and I started out, followed by Tom and Tom G., the porters behind with Effatta on his stretcher. Further back was the wheel-stretcher with the Japanese. The procession moved down the path that falls off from the Horombo Huts, which were quickly out of sight.

The trail moves southeasterly, crossing a ravine that runs through the side of the hill. Stu and I paused on the far rise of the ravine to look back as the porters ferrying the stretcher struggled through the mud of the stream bed.

At the Horombo Huts, January 1, 1984

In back of them the others pulled and pushed the wheel-stretcher with the Japanese. I wanted to take pictures of this riveting spectacle, but could not intrude overtly with a camera on the porters' efforts, or seem to make a sport of the gruesome drama of which we were a part. Pausing on the hill some distance above them, I ran a few feet of my movie camera.

Some Swedes were coming up the trail. They spoke excellent English, and we told them about the accident. The impact was immediate, because close behind was the body. They were not planning to go beyond the Horombo Huts. Later we saw two other groups; they had heard the news but had no details. After we filled them in, they said they would use the utmost care and would not attempt the top if the snow conditions were the same. Other than these few, we did not encounter people coming up. I learned later that as news of the accident spread below, some people hesitated to start the climb and that at the Gate itself people were turned back and the trail temporarily closed. Those we saw had started Saturday morning, before Jasper had reached the Gate with the news.

We continued for several hours, pausing a few times to rest. The stretchers continued to move at a steady rate, although the porters were straining where the trail turned up the side of a hill or dropped to cross a stream. The vegetation increased, but there were still extensive vistas which the weather had prevented us from seeing on the upward climb. Just before noon we followed the trail through thick woods as it came down on the side of a hill, took the course of a stream bed, and opened into the clearing at the Mandara Huts.

Meanwhile, Tom Jr., John, and Peter were almost at the Gate, while enormous blisters had forced Roland to stop at the Mandara Huts. Tom Jr. actually reached the Gate shortly after noon, with John and Peter close behind. Jasper, dressed in a shirt, green slacks, and high-heeled leather shoes—a far cry from his porter clothes—was at the Gate and came forward to meet them.

"Say, Jasper, how are you doing?" John called. "You came down yesterday?"

"Yes," said Jasper, grinning. "Four hours."

John said in surprise, "Four hours?"

Jasper smiled and with deserved pride held up four fingers.

John: "The porters are bringing the body down."

Jasper: "Yes, very bad, very bad."

It was New Year's Day, and a large number of well-dressed young people sat on the bench rails on both sides of the Gate. They seemed to know all about the accident.

At the Mandara Huts, crowds of Africans and European hikers were resting on the ground when Stu and I arrived. Roland, stoic and uncomplaining, was airing his feet. Stu stretched out on the grass and I sat in the shade of the main hut and ate the biscuit Effatta had given me. The sun was hot. A young porter, perhaps seventeen, had taken off his shirt and was wearing only shorts and boots. As he stepped over a pack his magnificently flowing muscles glistened in the sunlight. Soon the body arrived and was put on the ground some distance in front of the main hut, near where the trail starts to descend. The sick Japanese, who appeared comatose, was lifted off his stretcher, and laid out on the grass in the shade.

A lanky middle-aged African wearing a straw hat, white shirt, and slacks, came up the trail with several others, and stopped as he saw the body. It was Effatta's brother. Tom and Tom G. then arrived. We all were introduced and expressed our sympathy. Effatta's brother, who spoke no

English, was a gentle, courteous man and had come with extra hands to help carry the stretcher.

Those carrying the Japanese got ready to move again, and I cringed seeing his body jolted as the wheel of the stretcher moved over the rough ground. His eyes were closed and it was hard to tell if he was conscious; with relief I saw his hand close on one of the stretcher bars to steady his body. The porters picked up Effatta and we started down again.

Roland had gone ahead and Stu and I soon left Tom and Tom G. behind. The stretchers proceeded at a steady pace but Stu and I got ahead of them, and those carrying Effatta soon passed the Japanese. Stu said Effatta was like the hero of a Greek tragedy, his pride and confidence—his very virtues—leading to his fall. This was true, but there was added the fact of bad luck, and the element of fluke.

In less than an hour we came upon several more Africans ascending with a wheel-stretcher. They transferred Effatta's body to it. It was becoming clear that the repercussions from the tragedy were now resounding forcefully down the mountain, and that preparations were underway for our arrival at the Gate. With the wheel-stretcher and still more porters to assist, Stu and I soon realized we would have to move faster to keep ahead. The Africans began to handle the stretcher in shifts, four on and four off, and over parts of the trail they started to move at a jog. We could hear their chatter with the banging of the stretcher behind us, and, as if being chased, we were almost running to stay in front. On the steep descents we pulled ahead because they had to lift the body down, but on level stretches they closed the gap. The Japanese was not far behind, and I hated to think how he was being tossed about.

About an hour and a half below the Mandara Huts, and

still some miles above the Gate, we came upon a Landrover pickup truck. Three Africans had managed to drive it up the trail to meet us. The truck completely blocked the trail—I am still uncertain how they got it turned around for the trip down. Effatta's body was untied from the stretcher and, still in its olive shroud, lifted into the open back. The canvas of the stretcher, now empty in the hot sun, was wet and one end bloody. Again I wanted to photograph the extraordinary scene but felt it would be unseemly to do so, especially with Effatta's brother nearby. Soon the Japanese arrived and was unstrapped from his stretcher. He was semiconscious, and the Africans had trouble lifting his thick sagging body, the head rolling to the side, into the cab. There he was propped up, a porter on either side to hold him.

Fred told me to ride in the back and that Stu would have to walk. Tired as he was, he set off without complaint. I did not see the sick man's companion. Another Japanese hiker, an older man in his fifties whom I had seen several times on the trail, passed on his way down. He walked by the truck without the least sign of concern for his countryman. When we passed him a little later, he stood to the side as the truck went by, looking vacantly at us.

I climbed onto the left side panel of the truck, and sat in front near the cab where I could hold on to the roof. Nine other Africans pushed on to the back as well, including Effatta's brother who sat opposite me. Several packs and other items of equipment were also thrown in, although the stretchers were left behind. The driver climbed into the cab with the porters who held the sick man.

As the Landrover lurched down the trail, tilting precariously as one wheel or another rolled over a boulder, I tried to keep my feet clear so I could jump if we overturned. But Effatta's head and right shoulder kept sliding against my feet. Bushes and tree branches scraped the top of the cab, sometimes snapping back at me after being pushed ahead by the windshield, and a constant lookout was necessary to protect my face. For half an hour this hazardous ride continued, the Africans chattering calmly, a few puffing cigarettes. Eventually the trail widened and smoothed out, and about three o'clock, we reached the Gate.

There were crowds on either side as we drove out through the Gate and to the park headquarters buildings. We came to a stop in the large driveway and I saw Frank in his Volkswagen. He said the younger men had arrived on time and he had taken them to the Kibo Hotel. He knew all about the accident, and that I would have to go to the police station with the body. He said he would take the others to the hotel and wait for me there.

I gave Frank my stick to return to Godfrey and walked up and down in the hot sun while the Africans moved the sick man into another truck. This seemed to require extended discussion. There was further delay while they brought over jerry cans, and, with transparent hoses, siphoned gasoline into the truck. This too required much discussion. All the while, the unconscious man was propped up in the cab of the truck. A large number of people—all Africans—were in the area. Some of them seemed to be staying overnight in the building used as a lodge, the windows of which faced us. Yet they did not appear to be hikers; in fact, I did not see a single African hiker—other than the porters and guides—at any time on the mountain. These spectators were watching quietly and intently. Being the only white man in sight, and from my muddy boots and attire obviously one of those involved with the tragedy, I felt quite conspicuous. I am ashamed to say I enjoyed being for a few minutes the object of their attention, like an actor in a dark drama. Eventually the

Africans got enough gas into the sick man's truck and drove off to the Moshi hospital, twenty miles away. The sick Japanese was helpless and unattended by any of his countrymen.

It was necessary, apparently, to gas up our Landrover. This took another ten or fifteen minutes. Fred then told me to get in the cab. At the same time, several Africans climbed in the back with the body. The driver was from park headquarters, and spoke English quite well. He said he was in charge of getting us to the police, and the body to the hospital. I asked him if he knew Effatta's wife, and he said that he knew of her. I explained that we would like to visit her, to express our regrets, but that we were leaving in a few hours and would have to do so that afternoon. He thought one of Effatta's brothers, or perhaps sons, had told her of Effatta's death, but that it was possible she did not yet know. He did not think, however, it would do much good to see her if she did know because she would be too upset. He suggested that we send her a "purse" because she would appreciate money more than sympathy. It bothered me that the first note struck should be a financial one, but he was right. The pervasive poverty of the Africans leaves them with the single thought of asking for money or clothes as the first priority. I asked him whether others had been hurt or killed in similar snow conditions. He said that a Finnish hiker had slid to his death a year before but that the man had deliberately tried sliding and lost control.

We came to a crossroads and turned left, into the Himo Police Station, less than halfway to Moshi. I had expected to go to Moshi and, unaware of the exact distance, had not realized that the nearest police station was at the hamlet of Himo. The low cement building stood alone at the side of the road. It was sunbaked and partly open, with a porch across the front. There were flowers along the edge of the building and others in a row parallel to the road. The otherwise bright scene was dulled by barbed wire which enclosed the outer perimeter of the property, leaving only a central entrance for vehicles.

The park ranger, Fred, Felix, and I, with Effatta's brother, entered the building. A long counter divided the visitor's area from the rest of the room, which was bare and empty except for a single desk on the far wall. A policeman in a neat, clean uniform, his massive arms bulging from his short shirt sleeves, came to the counter. The park ranger and Fred explained in Swahili why we were there, whereupon the policeman went into a smaller office at the end of the room and telephoned, I assume, his superior. It was not every afternoon that a truck brought a corpse from the mountain. In a short time, an older man in casual shirt and trousers appeared and discussed the matter with the others. He had probably come from home and seemed to be the top local authority. Fred told me that he and I and Felix would fill out the police report while the park ranger and the others took the body to Moshi. They would come back later and return us to the Kibo Hotel. The big policeman hauled a large book from a shelf under the counter and, with Fred and Felix providing the information, wrote out all the details of the accident. The conversations being in Swahili I was at a loss, except to nod agreeably when it was obvious that Fred, pointing to me, was explaining that I was an eyewitness. When the long entry was completed, Fred and Felix signed. I was not asked to sign and, not being able to read the description, could not have done so.

We went out on the porch to wait for the truck. There were two or three Africans there besides Fred and Felix. It was hot but pleasant as we sat on the stone railings of the porch. The Africans chatted, smoking as usual, but I could not participate in their conversation. I took a swig from my canteen and Fred came over and borrowed it for a drink himself. This was the only time any of the Africans had asked to drink from my canteen but I would not have dreamt of refusing Fred, and I am sure he would have been astonished and hurt if I had. Soon Fred and the others went across the road to the "Mt. Kilimanjaro Bar and Restaurant," a small building emitting a stream of music.

It was a lazy Sunday afternoon, and, incongruously, New Year's Day. Up and down the road there was a constant flow of people, most in their twenties and thirties. They moved in and out of the bar and stood in groups to chat in the street. The sunny, dusty scene was the same as in rural communities anywhere, including the American South. It was a long way from the snowy heights of the mountain. A jeep drove up with two policemen and two drunks they had arrested. One staggered out of the car; the other fell out. When he could not or would not get up, one of the policemen grabbed his shirt and dragged him over the dirt and gravel and up the two stone steps of the building. Later a pregnant woman walked into the compound, escorted by a younger woman. The first was agitated and seemed to have been crying. After they entered, I went and looked in the door. The drunks were leaning toward the wall, their hands pressed against it, and were being searched. A policeman I had not previously seen, who must have come from the back of the building, was listening to the pregnant woman's complaint. I had the impression she was telling him someone had been hitting her. One of the policemen saw me watching and waved me outside.

Out on the porch again, I saw a few chickens come around the side of the building. Shortly, a little girl of six or seven came running after them. She scooted along gleefully until she looked up and saw me. This stopped her in her tracks; she stared in astonishment, then turned and ran back out of sight. In no time four other children peeped around the edge of the building. They then disappeared, to return with six older children, some in their teens. All looked at me in amazement, as at a sideshow freak. When I smiled, they quickly retreated out of sight. In Moshi no one gave me a passing glance, nor did they at the Kibo Hotel or at the Gate. But here, at a country spot in between, a white hiker, alone, must have been a rare phenomenon. For lack of transportation, these children had not seen many white men close up, and probably never at the police station.

Two men came to the building but I could not tell their errand. Looking at them, I noticed a poster on the wall with the picture of a Japanese man. The notice below, written in English, Japanese, and Swahili, reported that he had been missing for several months and gave an address for anyone knowing his whereabouts to contact.

The time dragged on. A kindly man in his fifties, in casual clothes, sat on the porch with me. He spoke little English. I learned he was a police sergeant on duty and not, as I had supposed, just a visitor. He asked me how much my boots cost in the United States. I was embarrassed to tell him $65 U.S., which to him was a fortune, but I would not have felt right shading the matter. To put things in context I told him that while pay was high in the United States, prices were high also, so one did not come out ahead. I refrained from saying that the boots were the cheapest ones on display when I bought them, and that most hiking boots cost a lot more. He asked to try on my sunglasses and seemed startled at their effect. The two men came out and walked off holding hands, which struck me as peculiar until I remembered that it is commonplace in Africa.

Fred and Felix returned, bringing me a mango. I had no

knife and was anxious to get at the juicy fruit, so I used the pin of my belt, which is like a key. With this I stabbed at the tough green rind, clumsily gouging the fruit open. I asked Fred if I could take his picture and moved out front to get a good shot. Fred immediately told me that it is against the law to take pictures of police stations, so I gave it up.

We talked about Effatta's family. Fred repeated what I had heard, that Effatta had three sons. I asked about Livingstone and was told he was not Effatta's son. Fred shook his head in disgust at what I had been told at the Kibo Hut. The news startled me because no one had denied it at the time. I was more than a little annoyed at Livingstone for having assumed the role thrust upon him, if he understood what I had been told. He may not have appeared on Sunday out of fear I had already learned the truth. The news made it necessary to change Effatta's eulogy to delete the reference to Livingstone, so taking the little book from my day pack, I altered the last page to read:

We extend our deep sympathy to his wife and family. We can understand their great loss but we know they will remember a loving husband and a father of whom they were proud.

At last the truck arrived and we headed for the Kibo Hotel. It was 5:30. The roads were still full of people, the women in colorful dresses, many carrying baskets or stalks of bananas on their heads. Most people, however, were not on errands but just out for a stroll and for society. With generally beautiful weather, and probably no destination as lovely as the roadside itself, the Tanzanians socialize by walking and stopping to talk. Their bright colors fill the roadside like flowers. For mile after mile the people appeared hospitable and friendly, as if at an extended block party.

As we moved upward toward the Kibo Hotel, I felt the time was near to ask the park ranger why hikers were not warned of the need for crampons and ice axes. This had been the first matter on my mind since Effatta fell, but I knew it would be taken as a criticism and had decided to postpone the subject until the end of the ride. Putting it as gently as I knew how, I suggested that perhaps the park authorities, or the custodian at Kibo Hut, could tell hikers they needed crampons when there was snow on the summit approaches. This remark drew an immediate defensive response. "Many people would not be able to have crampons," the ranger replied in an irritated tone that left no doubt the subject could not be profitably pursued. Even now I can make no sense of his comment. He must have been attributing a startlingly high priority to reaching the summit if he would fail to warn of the danger, because hikers might have to turn back for lack of the equipment necessary to save their lives. He might also have had the sense that crampons or ice axes were expensive, and hikers ought not to be disappointed in climbing just for lack of them. Or perhaps there were other explanations for his attitude, but they eluded me. On this note, we arrived at the Kibo Hotel.

Chapter 14
Homeward

Crowds of hikers, porters, and guides blocked the hotel entrance when I climbed down from the Landrover. This was the backflow from the Gate after the trail was closed. John was there. "Mom is sick," he told me calmly, trying not to create alarm. "She and the others are at Arusha. Uncle Tom will tell you about it. He just talked to Ellen."

Tom came through the crowd. "Mary Lee has a rash and fever, which started in Zanzibar," he said. "They got to Arusha Friday and are waiting at the Hotel 77."

I hurried through the crowd into the hotel. Godfrey was in his office talking to Effatta's brother and several other men. He greeted me gravely, "It has been bad luck. I am sorry you had such bad luck." I told him everything had been perfect until the moment Effatta fell, and asked him to express our sorrow to Effatta's brother.

Since I wanted to leave immediately, and this was the only chance to tell Effatta's family the details of the accident—there was now no time to see his wife—I explained, with Godfrey translating, exactly what had happened. However painful, it is necessary and even consoling to know in detail how a relative died, especially in an accident. Knowing helps one to share in the trauma, to be in spirit at the victim's side. Effatta's wife and family, if never provided these details, would be haunted unsparingly by speculation as to how it had all happened. I gave as precise an account as I would have wanted in their place. Effatta's brother thanked me. I said I was sorry not to see Effatta's wife, but my own wife was ill and I had to go to her immediately. Then I gave Godfrey Effatta's notebook and pictures, to be returned to his wife. Before handing these over, I inquired still again about Livingstone. Godfrey did not know Livingstone by name but said he was certain he was not Effatta's son. He did not even turn to ask Effatta's brother, and so I was confident he was sure of his answer. As we parted, Godfrey said that after we had time to get over the "bad memories" perhaps we would come back and climb again. I said "perhaps," and in my own mind did not rule it out. I shook hands with him and with Effatta's brother.

Heading out I saw the emotionless face of Livingstone. I mustered a courteous but noneffusive handshake, hoping he was not due more. As I reached the driveway, I remembered that I had checked a large bag of belongings in Godfrey's storeroom—not only some of my clothes but Mary Lee's and Ellen's, too. I rushed back to Godfrey, who got out his keys, giving one to the single assistant he appeared to trust with such matters, and I went to the storeroom on the floor above. The plastic sack, bigger than a trunk, had all the clothes and accessories we had not needed for the mountain, and the coats and clothes Mary Lee and Ellen had not needed for Zanzibar. We would not have been able to return for them had I forgotten, and I realized how affected I was by the turmoil and excitement.

Lugging these things outside, I was carrying my regular shoes by the laces when Fred came up, reached out, and said, "Give me shoes." That the man who had so commendably taken charge and brought us down from the mountain should now beg for shoes disturbed and saddened me. My instinct was to say, "No, Fred, this is beneath you—we will help you in some other way." But the moment was gone, I was moving quickly, and all I managed was, "I'm sorry, I need them." He withdrew, showing no emotion. I did not see him or any of our porters again.

In two vans we headed for Arusha. Tom and I were with Frank, with Stephen's van behind. As we neared Moshi, Stephen's van disappeared. He had detoured to stop briefly at his home where his family was having New Year's dinner. This hardly delayed his group and they arrived in Arusha only a few minutes behind us. I thought well of Stephen for this minor diversion but was glad that Frank, knowing how anxious I was, did not do the same.

It was dark when we reached Arusha. Ellen met us in the lobby and had everything in order, pleasantly explaining to the clerk who we were and what rooms should be assigned to us. This is not a simple task in Africa, with twelve people and the need for particular room assignments. The clerks, although their English is quite good, are not dealing in their native tongue.

Mary Lee was pale and drained; the rash covered her face and body, and was in her mouth and ears. Many of the splotches were infected sores. My arrival, filthy though I was, and the excitement and relief now that the men were finally on the scene, lifted her spirits, and after the initial shock I was relieved to see her perk up. I sat on the side of the bed, unaware that I had not washed for six days and was wearing the same clothes as when I left her.

She told me they had learned that morning that a KLM agent was stationed in Arusha. Ellen reached him at home. He was John Simpson, an Englishman, and Ellen's eyes had filled with tears of relief at the sound of his intelligent and comprehending English voice. He quickly appreciated the situation and had assured her that although the Monday night flight was full, he would arrange a place for Mary Lee when the plane stopped on its way to Amsterdam. He said he could get only one seat, but Ellen had told him Mary Lee was too ill to fly alone.

Later, Simpson's wife, a beautiful young Dutch woman,

several months pregnant, came to the room bringing medicines. Her spontaneous generosity, like that of the Maryknoll nuns, had made a deep impression.

Ellen had then telephoned Godfrey at the Kibo Hotel to tell him of Mary Lee's illness and explain that they were in Arusha and not at the Ngorongoro Lodge. Godfrey said that the hikers were delayed because a guide had been killed on the mountain. "My gosh," said Alice, "do you suppose it could have been a guide for our group?"

Although her fever had subsided, which reassured me greatly, Mary Lee still seemed dangerously ill. I did not appreciate how dehydrated she was or her constant need for fluid. The room was full of empty ginger ale bottles, the once-a-day cleanup being inadequate in the circumstances and the clean-up girls, having caught a glimpse of her the day before, being afraid to enter the room. Mary Lee had heard them talking and had caught the Swahili words for "European woman" and "sick."

The phone rang. It was Greg, Ellen's husband, calling her from New York, where it was still early afternoon. As they talked and Mary Lee rested, I showered, shaved, and put on clean clothes for dinner.

The dining room was spacious and even elegant, with a distinct African flavor. The maitre d' was neatly suited, and the waiters were in uniform. In the center of the room, which was broken up by buffet tables and waiters' stands, was a willowy African Christmas tree, with sparkling strings of tinsel and small lights. It had an exotic attractiveness, like a skinny woman with straight hair in a flapper dress from the twenties. Across one wall was a "Merry Christmas and Happy New Year" streamer. Our group was seated at a long table; in his sport coat and tie, Tom would hardly have been recognized by those who had seen him earlier that day on the mountain. In another section of the

180

room was a large table of Japanese. I did not recognize any of them from the mountain and so did not inquire about the sick man. The food was tasty but I lacked the snappy appetite of the climb; nevertheless, it felt good to be at a clean table, with lights, and in a comfortable chair. After dinner, everyone went to Mary Lee's room. The company was enlivening and, despite her condition, she laughed and chatted and was buoyed by the banter and companionship.

John and Peter lingered after the others left. Peter said he cried the night after the accident, thinking what might have happened if he had not stopped my slide. I felt tears in my own eyes and put my arms around his powerful shoulders.

Mary Lee had a restless night, constantly needing fluid. Again, I slept soundly, to my surprise. John and Peter knocked to say hello on their way to breakfast, and after ordering toast and tea for Mary Lee, I joined the others in the dining room. They were all in a happy mood, looking ahead to the safari. There was a sense that the trauma of the preceding week was now a closed chapter and that a new, safer adventure was in prospect. Even in less challenging circumstances, it occurred to me that much is to be gained by dividing a vacation into distinct segments, so that if one is unpleasant it will soon be superseded, and if one is good it will provide fond memories before it is allowed to spoil.

Fred and Stephen arrived and the packs and luggage were loaded in the van. Everyone went to say goodbye to Mary Lee and to wish her luck. I gave Peter and John my cameras, binoculars, and additional money; Tom was designated "leader" of the group, since every group must have a leader when traveling in Tanzania; then we all hugged and shook hands. Tom G. said somberly: "I know how disappointed you are not to be going with us." But I was so anxious to get Mary Lee to reliable doctors that I had no sense of disappointment.

I telephoned the KLM office. John Simpson said that he could get us both on the flight that night. I had hoped, in view of Mary Lee's illness, that we would still be entitled to our original group fare, the difference being several thousand dollars. He said he did not know if that could be arranged and that Ellen had said we would pay whatever was necessary. I told him that was in fact true. He said to bring our tickets to his office and he would complete the arrangements. I took a cab to the downtown area of Arusha, which was not far away but which was unfamiliar territory. The main street, while dusty and by no means modern, was more impressive than Moshi. It resembled a small prairie town on the midwestern plains, but with an African flavor, and, of course, almost all black faces. At the KLM office I found several African women, neatly dressed, sitting at desks. They pointed me to Simpson's office in the back. He was a man in his late thirties or early forties, handsome, efficient, and pleasant. I thanked him for his wife's visit to Mary Lee, which I said had meant a great deal to her. He made light of it and said he would be glad to take care of the ticket arrangements and seating. He did inquire, however, exactly what was wrong with Mary Lee. I explained that it was expected that it was an allergic reaction, rather than a contagious disease, pointing out that we had only been a week in Africa and that this was the diagnosis of the medical missionary, who had consulted by phone with our doctors in New York. I said that arrangements had been made for her to go directly to the hospital as soon as we arrived home.

Simpson left his office briefly to take care of the tickets and came back a few minutes later, handing me tickets that showed that we were on the flight. He also told me that we would be able to have the same fare and that he wanted to reconfirm, while I was there, the names of the rest of the group who would be departing a week later. When these matters were taken care of, I told Simpson how much we appreciated his courtesy and cooperation. I then mentioned, for the first time, that my law firm in New York is counsel for KLM in the United States. Naturally he was surprised, and I trust pleased, to know that he had been able to help us.

I decided to check with Mr. Lilla about a refund because Mary Lee and I would not be going on safari. The Tourist Office had one large room with eight or ten desks and travel personnel; business seemed inexplicably brisk. Mr. Lilla was at his desk, smiling and courteously soft-spoken as before. I suggested that in our circumstances it would be good business for the Tanzanian Tourist Board to refund the safari part of the price. He said that he did not know if that would be possible, but he would look into the matter and be in touch with me. I also told him that we had to square the hotel bill at the Hotel 77, where our group spent extra nights because of the change in plans. He said to tell the hotel to send him the bill and he would take care of it. He also arranged for a taxi that would take us to the airport that night. He was very apologetic for the trouble and difficulty we had had, which I told him was not his fault as far as the climbers were concerned, although he did have some responsibility for sending the women to Zanzibar, without warning of the problems there. I told him that no tourist should be sent to Zanzibar because conditions getting there, staying there and, most of all, getting out of there were not consistent with an American's idea of a vacation. He nodded in agreement—he seemed born to agree—but I doubted that my words had much effect.

Walking down the street, whom did I spy but the glum

Canadians and their friend. The former wore their every-day resigned expressions; their friend, his chronic smile. They seemed to insist on having a bad time and he a good time. I stopped to say hello and told them how our climb had ended in tragedy. The woman said nothing, the smiling one was also silent, and the man, in the pompous tone he had used before, said, "Yes, we heard it was hairy up there." I often wondered how—or why—they came to Tanzania.

Up the street I found a bookstore and leafed without understanding through several volumes in Swahili. Further on was the Arusha Hotel, which is more inviting than the Hotel 77 or the hotel in Moshi. It encloses a large garden, where a colorful variety of Africans and Europeans—including a bearded man in white hunter attire—were strolling. In the lobby, one of the shops featured every size of carved animals. It was run by a white woman, who spoke sharply when I inquired about the price of one of the objects. I could not tell if she was German or Swiss; probably the former, the German influence being still strong in Arusha.

It was a pleasant day, and I walked back along a wide boulevard heavily traveled by pedestrians. The street and the open field on one side were dusty, but it was a country dust, not the dirt of a city. Set back from the street on the other side, behind columns of trees, were large houses. I could not tell whether they were used for commercial purposes or as apartments. They were not new and belonged to the more prosperous colonial period.

Mary Lee was still dehydrated and suffering from the infected sores. But there was nothing to be done except to move the ginger ale bottles out front. I tried reading but could not concentrate. At noon I ordered her lunch and went into the dining room, where an elaborate buffet was available. I took some cow stew, rice, and bread, but de-

184

cided against the unidentifiable vegetables. There were a number of Japanese having lunch, and a few others who appeared to be American or English. I studied the Japanese but did not recognize any of them. Finally, I asked one whether he knew anything about the sick man. He dismissed me brusquely, saying he knew nothing.

Later in the afternoon, I gathered our first aid supplies and delivered them at the front desk of the hotel. Mary Lee had told Sister Genevieve that we would leave them for her, the least we could do to reciprocate. An hour later, when I had moved our luggage to the front, I learned that the nuns had already appeared and collected the package. Thinking we had left, they had not called.

Checking out, I found the bill incomprehensible. It had a fistful of attachments showing charges for drinks and other extras, including all the phone calls for our group. The cashier was both impatient and unwilling to explain the bill and, although purporting to speak English, had difficulty understanding me. I finally told her that Mr. Lilla of the Tourist Office had said the bill should be sent to him. I wrote that on the bill and she took it with no further questions.

About 6:30 our cab appeared, filled with Africans. The driver leaned out of the window, asked my name, assured me, "Oh, yes, I'll be right back," and took off again. While waiting I noticed a large truck—almost as big as a truck used for earth moving—parked near the front of the hotel. It was a safari company van to carry tourists in the wilds. The steel sides permit tourists to stand up, look over the bulwarks, and take pictures of animals close up. The cab returned and Mary Lee slowly made her way out.

Perhaps 150 travelers—all shockingly white when seen in one place—were at the airport check-in when we arrived. Simpson appeared in a KLM uniform, with a white

185

shirt and blue epaulets. He gave our bags to one of the KLM attendants with instructions to check them through to New York. Then he took our tickets and disappeared. I saw the big policeman who, the day before, had taken the report of Effatta's death; he was also in a KLM uniform, checking baggage. Simpson arranged for us to have the front seats on the left of the plane; this gave us the maximum space and privacy. Over the protests of the crowd waiting to go through the checkpoint into the customs area, he escorted Mary Lee and me to the front. Concealing my embarrassment, I made elaborate gestures to indicate my wife was ill. But their hoots were loud and friendly.

Everyone was searched thoroughly in the customs section—which was a no-man's land with partitioned cubicles between the check-in area and the waiting room. Men were ushered into booths on one side and women into booths on the other. In each booth an attendant required that pockets and handbags be emptied, and then searched each person. The attendant insisted on seeing all of my money, and wanted to take my Tanzanian shillings. I protested, to which he replied, "What good will they do you— you're leaving, give them to me." But I demurred, saying that I might come back sometime—a statement he rarely heard, I imagine. When he saw that I would not give in, he relented and passed me through.

In the waiting room there were plenty of seats. We got ginger ale and rested. The room is at ground level, providing a full view of the runway. Before long I saw the lights of the KLM plane. It was a beautiful sleek DC-8 stretch and was a welcome sight. Simpson went out and climbed the steps; when the cabin door opened, he shook hands with the attendant. Then I saw the crisply uniformed Dutch steward and stewardesses. Simpson brought the steward in and introduced us, explaining that the steward would be in charge to Khartoum and would take care of us. He was a handsome Dutchman named Guido Coemerick, and he shook hands pleasantly. Mary Lee nodded but kept most of her face covered.

The food and service were excellent, and the steward kept us under a watchful eye. About 2:00 A.M. we reached Khartoum. Here the crew changed. Before he left, Coemerick introduced us to the new steward, Loomans, who in turn assisted us to Amsterdam. During the night, in which no one seemed to sleep, an African who had boarded at Khartoum and was sitting across the aisle asked if I had any Tanzanian shillings to sell. Surprised, I told him I would be happy to sell what I had at 12 shillings to the dollar. He proceeded to give me U.S. dollars. I did not know until months later that in New York $1.00 will buy 33 Tanzanian shillings. I offered him a stick of chewing gum; he politely took the pack to select a stick, and then pocketed the pack. Relieved to have exchanged the money, I did not protest. Mary Lee slept intermittently and feasted on the water, available for the first time on the aircraft. Shortly after dawn we reached Vienna and, about 8:00, we landed in Amsterdam.

As we came off the plane, a KLM representative met us and escorted us to a rest center where beds can be rented for stopovers. But no beds were available until noon, so I found a wheelchair and took Mary Lee to the first-aid room. A doctor examined her and said that she could continue to New York, especially if she could go immediately into the hospital there. He gave us antihistamine tablets and aspirin in case her fever returned. We spent the next few hours resting in the airport waiting room. About 1:45, I took her in a wheelchair to the gate. Here the passengers were mostly Americans, and we began to feel in familiar surroundings.

Seated in front of us on the plane was a charming woman with the interesting name of Shannon St. John. She and her friends had been on safari and Shannon had been sick, like Mary Lee, although she had recovered in a few days. She agreed it might be an allergic reaction to the malaria pills and diarrhea medicine. I asked Shannon if she had heard anything about our accident. She had not, but she had heard that a Japanese climber had died from altitude sickness at the Moshi hospital the day before. This must have been the man who came down with us. I was distressed at the fate of the poor Japanese, and stung by the realization that if he had been brought down sooner, he might have survived. It was an awful feeling to now know how ignorant we were Saturday night at the Horombo Huts, failing to appreciate that the sick man was dying because others—ourselves included—were resting instead of getting him to a lower elevation. It is so easy to read warnings about getting down and to think one understands them but only the branding iron of experience, the searing hurt of knowing that one could have helped but failed, drives the message home.

Mary Lee continued to drink water constantly. I slept briefly but was cramped and full of aches. I wondered how I would manage my pack and Mary Lee's bag when we got to the hospital.

Lyndon Johnson once referred to a companion as "a man I'd go to the well with."

"What do you mean by that, Mr. President?" a reporter asked him.

"Ya see," said Johnson, "in the old days, when the Indians had the place surrounded and you were holed up battling them off, you had to sneak out at night and crawl down to the well to get water. You always wanted with you the one person who was the most reliable, most trustworthy, most sure of being there and doing what needed to be done. He was the one 'you'd go to the well with.' "

Harriet Boyd Sedgwick, Vassar '38, of Scarsdale, New York, is someone you'd go to the well with. The day before we arrived, knowing nothing of our misadventures, she had telephoned George's wife to ask about Mary Lee's mother, who had been ill. Harriet learned that while her mother was doing well, Mary Lee herself was flying home to go directly to the hospital. That was enough for Harriet. As we emerged from customs, Mary Lee in a wheelchair pushed by a KLM attendant and I with our luggage, Harriet was waiting to take us to the hospital.

Dr. Cahill met us in the Lenox Hill Hospital emergency room. It was 6:00 P.M. and we had been traveling for thirty-two hours. He escorted Mary Lee quickly through the admissions office and upstairs to a room on a quiet corridor. There an IV was started to restore her fluid balance. Dr. Charles DeFeo, head of dermatology, came to examine her; he arranged for biopsies the next day. I had not grasped the seriousness of her condition. Dr. Cahill told me, "She's a very sick woman."

Harriet and I went to dinner at a nearby restaurant. Returning to the hospital, we found that Harriet's daughter, Sally, was with Mary Lee, who was cheered by this moral support and buoyed by the realization that she was finally home and in competent medical hands. As we left the hospital, Sally looked at me and said that her mother should drive to Scarsdale. I gave way easily, even though I generally do the driving. On the way up the Bronx River Parkway, I could not stay awake. Despite every effort to talk to Harriet, I repeatedly drifted off. When I finally climbed into bed, I had been up over forty-eight hours—a fitting home stretch after eleven days packed with half a lifetime's excitement, drama, and tragedy.

Chapter 15
Restored

Unaware of it, Mary Lee was moved the next morning to an isolation room. A sign outside the door warned off visitors; next to it was a hamper with gowns and gloves for medical attendants who found it necessary to enter. None of this was apparent to the patient and she was startled when a nurse and orderly, masked and garbed, came to tell her where she was. Then Dr. DeFeo arrived and lifted pieces of the infected sores for biopsy. The procedure was painless but made her shudder. Dr. Cahill stopped in but decided against medication pending the laboratory report. Although the IV was restoring her fluid balance, the next few days showed no improvement; she ran an erratic fever which did not conform to the usual day-night cycle.

On Wednesday things seemed reasonably encouraging because, although no better, Mary Lee was no worse. Greg came by that evening. He is a biochemist at New York University Hospital and made his own check of the medical records.

The lab tests received Thursday were inconclusive and additional tests, requiring another day, were necessary. There was further word that some of the "material" was being sent to a different lab. Mary Lee was uncomfortable, and frustrated because she was not being given any medication. Sitting in her room Thursday evening I suddenly felt tired and developed an ache across the back of my shoulders. We attributed this to the strain and the journey home.

The lab reports Friday provided essential but incomplete answers. They showed an allergic reaction, not a tropical disease, but did not pinpoint the precise cause. I felt it must have been the combination of the malaria and diarrhea medicines. Both contain sulphur, and the cumulative amount from taking both types of pills must have been too much. We had all taken the malaria pills for two weeks before we left for Africa, since that is the normal requirement. The diarrhea medicine, however, had been taken for the first time at the Kibo Hotel, and the rash appeared within forty-eight hours. But this was simply the broad picture. We had taken two types of malaria pills: Aralan, which is chloroquine, and Fansidar, a different drug. This was to guard against two strains of malaria currently prevalent in East Africa. Did both—or only one of them, in combination with Doxycline, the other medicine—cause the reaction? We could not be sure, which meant that Mary Lee must avoid both, and therefore future trips to malaria-infested countries.

Once the lab reports were in, Dr. Cahill prescribed steroids to combat the reactions. Mary Lee improved and was anxious to go home. She complained that nothing was being done for her in the hospital that could not be done at home and said she wanted to leave the next day. A dignified, soft-spoken man, the doctor closed the door, sat down on the bed and said, "I want to tell you something." He described the case of a forty-two-year-old woman who, on a trip to Africa, had developed the same illness. She returned to the United States on a holiday weekend and was taken to a hospital in upstate New York. She grew progressively worse. When finally brought to New York her fever was 105 degrees. It had not been possible to reverse the reaction and she had died.

"I am not going to let you out of here until we are certain that we have reversed your reaction, and that nothing more needs to be done. If everything goes smoothly, you may be able to leave on Sunday."

This satisfied her. But on Saturday she telephoned me at home in alarm. There had been another outbreak of rash, and new red splotches covered her body. More steroids were given. There was no hope of leaving the hospital Sunday.

In the next two days, however, the steroids began to win out. Tuesday morning I arrived at the hospital early, with Mary Lee more than ready to leave. She looked frightful but the rash and blotches were beginning to fade, and the infected sores were closing. Dr. DeFeo assured her that after the reaction itself had stopped, the sores would clear up and, in six to eight weeks, disappear.

Late that afternoon, the others arrived at Kennedy. I had Tom's car driven to the airport so he and his family could leave directly for Rochester, and sent a letter explaining that Mary Lee was recovering and had been brought home from the hospital.

It might be assumed that Tom headed north into a blizzard—which in fact prevented him from reaching Rochester until noon the next day—because he had pressing business, or because his sons needed to return to classes, or simply because they wanted to get home after their long trip. All of this was true but only part of the story. The real reason was more compelling, if less understandable, to those of us who did not go to Notre Dame. Notre Dame graduates, like the real Irish, are amiable but unbalanced in their primitive enjoyments. On December 30, Notre Dame had played Boston College in the Liberty Bowl. Before leaving for Africa, arrangements had been made for a neighbor to tape the game so that it could be shown on Tom's television as soon as they arrived. There was a determined effort on the flight home to insure that no one saw the *International Herald Tribune* or any other paper that might have the score. In the Amsterdam airport an Irish-American approached Tom Jr., who was wearing a Notre Dame cap; the man was immediately told to say nothing about Notre Dame football. It was the lure of the game that spurred the group forward.

John and Peter were full of their adventures on safari. Frank and Stephen had shown them thousands of animals. They had photographed, up-close, cheetahs, baboons and wildebeests, elephants, lizards, and lions. And the plains and game parks of Tanzania had proved wonderfully remote and primitive. The lodges, beautifully designed and built, had been lacking in supplies and almost deserted. They had felt in nineteenth-century Africa.

Tom Jr. had gotten sick at one of the lodges and had to remain behind, Alice staying with him. But they had eventually rejoined the group. Stu had predictable misadventures. He had purchased his hiking stick from Godfrey, and had asked Tom to carry it for him at one of the lodges. Somehow, it was left behind, and so the single physical memento of the tragic climb was lost. Stu also bought a large skin-covered shield from a Masai warrior on the plains—the type of shield used to protect against the charge of a lion. He had Frank bargain for a spear from another Masai in one of the villages. The shield and spear created a stir on the flight to Amsterdam, and again when Stu carried them aboard for the flight across the Atlantic. He refused, understandably, to let them out of his sight. On the last leg from New York to Washington, he was required to store them in the cockpit. They now adorn the living-room wall of his Maryland home.

My impression is that Tanzania is the place to go if you want to see the world's greatest herds of wild animals. Kenya is more prosperous and civilized. Its lodges are reportedly more elegant, and most Americans, when they talk of East Africa, mean Kenya. But Tanzania, with its more primitive accommodations, has the great advantage of more animals and of seeing them unsurrounded by crowds. Our group saw few other people in the great animal parks; those who have been to Kenya tell of many vehicles out watching the animals. Thus, I would choose Tanzania, cruder, rougher, with nature more in the raw.

In the weeks that followed, Mary Lee slowly recovered. The steroid dosages were continually reduced, and after a month were stopped entirely. By early February, she began again to feel normal. With recovery came a new appreciation of life and good health, and a clear awareness—which a crisis demonstrates—of the difference between the important and the inconsequential.

My own fatigue and aching shoulders were, it turned out, not attributable to worry or exhaustion. A few days after Mary Lee returned from the hospital I, too, visited Dr. Cahill. Appropriate samples were taken, and lab tests showed I had brought home a stowaway African amoeba. It had been vacationing in my bloodstream, feasting insatiably, and causing aches and fatigue. Ten days of pills were prescribed. After nine days, I was about to call Dr. Cahill to say that I felt no worse but no better. However, that morning I was in the Federal Court of Appeals, for oral argument in an important antitrust case. Before my turn came, I sat listening to the opposing lawyer. He was being assailed by questions from the three judges, and I reveled in the difficulty he had in trying to answer them. Suddenly, as I was watching, I felt physically fine; in a single instant I knew that my foreign guest had been dispatched. It was an extraordinary feeling, this immediate and definite restoration to verve and strength.

After she recovered, Mary Lee called the Westchester

County Medical Society to describe her experience, suggesting that people be warned against mixing malaria and diarrhea drugs. Her reaction, it turned out, had not been unique. Over a year later, the Travel Section of *The New York Times* had the following announcement:

MALARIA MEDICATION. Concerned about serious adverse reactions to use of the drug Fansidar, the Federal Centers of Disease Control has stopped uniformly recommending it for travelers to areas with strains of malaria resistant to chloroquine. Previously the centers had recommended the combined use of chloroquine and Fansidar.

The areas involved include much of sub-Sahara Africa, South America, the Indian subcontinent and Southeast Asia. Travelers planning to visit those areas are strongly advised, before leaving home, to consult their physicians for the best recommendations consistent with their personal medical histories. Guidance for physicians is available from the centers, which are in Atlanta.*

The problem, of course, is that some travelers, like Mary Lee, had never before reacted to drugs so there was no way to predict such consequences. If alerted, however, one would know to stop the medicine and head for home if such a reaction occurred.

Mary Lee also had our church include in its Sunday bulletin a request for medical supplies for the Maryknoll nuns who had helped her. The response was immediate and plentiful. She took the donations to the Maryknoll Mother House in Ossining, New York. There a brother, working in a warehouse, packs supplies of all kinds—furniture, motorcycles, medicine, clothing—for shipment abroad. It is not practical to send such things directly to the missionary outposts, because they are invariably stolen in transit. Instead, they are packed into large trailers, the size of moving vans, then locked, sealed, and sent by sea. This takes months but ensures safe and economical, if delayed, delivery. In Tanzania, as in other countries, there is the added problem of getting supplies inland from the ocean ports. Mary Lee had requested that some of the supplies be taken from Dar es Salaam to Arusha, but she never learned whether they arrived safely.

Chapter 16
The Elusive Cave

In writing this story, I wanted to determine the place at which Effatta fell. This I had estimated to be 1,000 slope feet above the Cave, but none of the maps or route descriptions gave the Cave's altitude. They referred to it as "halfway" between Kibo Hut and Gillman's Point, but the great variation in the angle of ascent made this too indefinite.

I went first to the New York Public Library. In the reference room I found the 1971 edition of a *Guide to Mt. Kenya and Kilimanjaro,* published by the Mountain Club of Kenya. This is an earlier version of the book the American had been reading at the Horombo Huts. His book, I thought, had a detailed color map, but the library book had only a small drawing, on which it was not possible to pinpoint the Cave. The book referred to Edward Stanford, Ltd., 12 Long Acre, London, as a map source, and to West-Col Productions, 1, Meadow Close, Goring, Reading, Berkshire, England, as distributors of the book outside Africa. Acting on the parochial premise that "if you can't buy it in New York, it doesn't exist," I called several bookstores, without success.

Unconcerned, I waited until a month later when Mary Lee and I went to London. There I called Edward Stanford, Ltd., for 150 years a seller of maps and guidebooks, and asked if they had a survey map of Kilimanjaro. The woman in the Map Department, with English acuteness, knew what I wanted. "Please hold on, we used to have a few such sheets; I'll just check the shelves." A moment later, with equal precision and finality, she told me, "Sorry, we used to have them but they are no longer available."

"No longer available." Her words had the resonance of history, and I sensed that the great infra-structure of British civilization, here reflected in so unlikely an item as a contour map, had began to crumble after Tanzanian independence. Hoping I was wrong, I called the Tanzania Tourist Office.

"Yes, we have a map of the hiking route; I believe we can help you," was the courteous reply.

The map did indeed turn out to be somewhat better than the one in the guidebook, but was no more useful for locating the Cave. Coming out from the Tourist Office, we paused on the steps to look at our map of London. An attractive woman stopped to ask if we needed directions. "No, we're looking for a contour map of Mt. Kilimanjaro," I replied smiling. To this statement she responded with aplomb:

"Why not try the National Geographic Society?"

"Do they have a place in London?" I asked, thinking of their headquarters in Washington.

"Well, perhaps it's called the British Geographic Society."

"The *Royal* Geographic Society," Mary Lee suggested.

"Ah, yes," the woman said, "that's it; it's on the road below Kensington Gardens and Hyde Park."

Thirty minutes later, we approached the venerable brick building which, since 1913, has been the society's headquarters. It has the quaint address of 1 Kensington Gore—the last word meaning, among other, less agreeable things, a triangular piece of land, to which I presume it once referred. In the nineteenth century, when major portions of the globe were still unexplored, the society was the launching pad for the great expeditions. These included the African explorations, especially those that sought the sources of the Nile. In this century, the society has supported, among others, Scott's First Antarctic Expedition, Shackleton's Trans-Arctic Expedition, and consecutive Mount Everest attempts, including Hillary's triumphant ascent in 1953.

In a recess on the outside wall is the figure of Livingstone, turning back one's thoughts even before one enters to the great explorers who returned to report their discoveries. In the days before television and radio, when a first-hand account could be heard only face to face, the meetings must have had a drama equalled in our time only by the telecast of the landing on the moon. Darwin came after his portentous voyage on the *Beagle*. Wallace, who separately conceived and more cogently stated the theory of national selection, lectured to the society. Speke returned to assert, to the disbelief of leading geographers, that he had discovered a great lake which was the origin of the Nile. Speke died, at thirty-seven, in a hunting accident in England before his discovery was accepted, but across the road in Kensington Gardens the monument I had seen years before contains his name alone of all those who searched for the source of the Nile.

The front doors of the building open into a reception hall. An attendant who was at a glass-enclosed desk asked us to complete a form indicating the reason for our visit. I checked the space for "Visitors," as distinguished from "Fellows," "Government Officials," and others more eminent. We were then directed to the Map Room, straight ahead. To the left was a wide corridor containing pictures, ship models, globes, and other fascinating display cases, all of which it required maximum concentration to ignore. But in these historic surroundings, as uninvited guests, we felt it prudent to proceed straight ahead with a purposeful attitude, concealing our real colors as fickle tourists, easily diverted by cheap gift shops—to say nothing of genuine artifacts from the ends of the earth.

The far wall of the Map Room has windows that reach to the ceiling, providing an elegant dimension and capturing fully the available light and sunshine. Thin deep drawers, with maps of every age and region, line the other walls and rows of wide-top tables, each with map drawers underneath, fill the center of the room. A railing parallels the side from which we entered, dividing most of the room from the visitor's area. An attendant took us to the card catalogue, locating the section on "Tanganyika, Kilimanjaro," and asked me to write on the back of our entrance form what maps I wanted to see. There were eight or ten listed and I felt a thrill holding the cards, most of which were dark with age:

1. Mt. Kilimanjaro by H. H. Johnston, 1884 (hand drawn).

2. Sketch Map of Mt. Kilimanjaro by Mr. H. H. Johnston; published for the proceedings of the Royal Geographic Society, 1885.

3. Ker Kibo-Krater des Kilimandscharo nach einer provisorischen, Skizze des Dr. Hans Meyer, Okt 1889.

4. The Kibo Crater from a sketch by Dr. Hans Meyer reduced from Petermann's Mitteilungen, Part 1, 1890.

5. Karte des Schneegebirges Kilima-ndjaro aufgenommen von Baron C. von der Decken (undated).

6. Spezialkarte des Kilima-ndsharo und Meru-Gebietes Dr. Hans Meyer, Lieut. L.V. Hohnel, Dr. Oscar Baumann, u.A., 1893.

There were more recent maps too, including "D.O.S. No. 522," published in 1965, which must have been the source for the map in the guidebook. "Ah," I thought, "the contour map I am after." Greedily I copied the list and handed it to the attendant. She said it would take a few minutes to assemble the sheets, because some of the older maps were stored in another room. We were asked to wait in the New Map Room farther down the hall. Dutifully we proceeded there, lingering now to examine the models and other displays in the hall.

The New Map Room is bright and spacious, with large bay windows that face a garden. There are several large tables for spreading maps. The architect of long ago was clearly unfamiliar with the constricting tendencies of modern design—those that compress the mind and spirit. He knew only how to provide light and grace, and a largeness of impression fitting for the adventures celebrated here.

To the left as one enters is a portrait of Livingstone, 1813–1873; he is in a frock coat and bow tie, looking strong and determined. Next is a huge "Map of the World, c. 1650," by Fr. Matteo Ricci, brought back from China long ago by an English seaman. In front of the window stands a model of Everest and its surrounding peaks. A plaque states that it was "presented in March 1953 by its makers, Cockade, Limited, later reconstructed on the basis of information provided by the Expedition on its return."

Henry Morton Stanley, in a portrait painted in Cairo in 1890, looks down from the opposite wall, and around a corner is a melange of arrows, darts, and small spears, "Relics of Emin Pasha Relief Expedition, 1887/9." Remarkably, there is a similar display in Dr. Cahill's office in New York. Stanley, who in 1871 had found Livingstone, several years later marched *from* the Atlantic Coast to find Pasha on Lake Albert. On another wall is a painting of "Capt.

Robert Falcon Scott, Died on the Barrier, March 1912, returning from the South Pole," and, next to him, a painting of "Captain James Cook, 1728–1779," discoverer of the Hawaiian Islands.

Just inside the entrance, opposite Livingstone, is an arresting portrait of Speke. He is standing on the lakeshore; behind him are the falls which he named for Lord Ripon, who, at the time of Speke's explorations, was the president of the Society. Speke has a full beard, and is wearing a wool shirt, tattersall hunting vest, grey pants, and black shoes. His rifle is leaning against a tree; he holds a compass and his sextant, with a telescopic sight, lies nearby on the grass. One sees that the artist has captured the pride that built an empire, for although standing in a remote and alien land, Speke remains, in dress and bearing, ever the English sportsman—of whom it is rightly said, "he is always in England." The plaque below the painting, reflecting the anonymity which has been Speke's fate, bears the full description:

Capt. John Hanning Speke, Discoverer of the Victoria Nyanza 1859, called by permission after Her Majesty Queen Victoria The Main Source of the Nile.

J. Witner Wilson

The attendant brought in the maps and I was trusted to examine them freely, although of some there can be few if any other copies. Johnson's 1884 map was hand-drawn, his name and the date written near the top. It had the society's receipt stamp, "21 Jul. 85." All the others were printed, the 1889 Hans Meyer map showing it had been received "23 Jan. 90." The 1893 Spezialkarte also had the receipt stamp of "24 May 93." Holding these aged charts, the records of prodigious efforts at altitudes never before achieved, and accomplished in lands as remote as the moon today, I felt I was almost touching the sleeves of the explorers. All but the earliest maps showed the route we had taken toward the summit, but none noted the Hans Meyer Cave. Nor, to my grievous disappointment, did the 1965 map, by far the largest and most detailed. Its contour lines were clear, but, despite my repeated examination of the scale and comparisons with the other maps, I could not determine the altitude of the Cave.

The attendant made me copies, except for the 1965 map, which she said was "protected by copyright." A printed note stated it was published for the United Republic of Tanzania by the Director of Overseas Surveys, and that copies could be obtained by writing to the Tanzania Ministry of Lands, Settlement, and Water Development in Dar es Salaam. It also stated that Edward Stanford and Sons were agents for distribution. These references were now almost two decades old. I knew the latter was no longer correct, and I doubted the former, too.

Foyle's, on Charing Cross Road, calls itself "the world's greatest bookshop," and purports to have a stock of "over four million volumes." Neither statement is an exaggeration; indeed, I would confidently—even smugly—say that one should not consider oneself literate who has not crawled around the warren of book-crammed rooms of this extraordinary establishment. When I first put Foyle's to the test some years ago, I went to the philosophy department on the fourth floor and said to the man at the inquiry desk, "Do you have a copy of Kant's *Critique of Pure Reason,* second edition, 1787?" Without turning his head he reached back and pulled forth a copy, handing it to me with no hint of triumph. Now I approached again, asking where I might find a guidebook to Mount Kenya and Mount Kilimanjaro. "Please go to the Sports Section on the third floor," I was told. Walking up, I found my way to the area marked "Africa," and, reaching up, pulled down a copy of the guide. Foyle's had done it again. This was the 1981 edition, but to my disappointment the map in the back was little different from the one I had already seen. The preface explained that the border between Kenya and Tanzania had been closed for some years, interfering with efforts to update the description of Kilimanjaro.

My hunt for the Cave's elevation was now becoming an obsession. The next week we were at the Springs Hotel, a country inn on the Thames, an hour west of London. Looking at a map I noticed we were only four miles from Goring, the address for West-Col Publications, distributors of the guidebook. Goring is a rural hamlet and hardly the location for an international book distributor. Nevertheless we drove down and, after some difficulty, finally found "1 Meadow Close." It was a brick house on a residential lane that had obviously changed drastically in the thirteen years since the guidebook was published. Searching through a phone book, I saw that West-Col was still in business, now with the even more puzzling address of "Copse Ho, Goring Hth." At the railroad station, the ticket agent translated the latter words as "Goring Heath," which he explained was, naturally, a different town eight miles north. Off we headed on a small country road, suspecting that our efforts were futile but now more than ever determined to run the quarry to the ground. We stopped at the first noticeable cluster of buildings that might, with an effort, be called a town. They bordered a school, where boys in emblemed sweaters and shorts were at soccer. I went in the pub—it being about noon—and asked the bartender for help. He and the two patrons, elderly men who appeared long in place on their stools, squinted at me uncomprehendingly. After two unsuccessful verbal sallies in our common language, I showed them the paper on which I had written the address. They immediately brightened. "Copse Ho" meant—of course—"Copse House," but what was I doing here? We could not miss it, they explained, unaware that I already had, because it was at the next crossroads and the post office was there. Retracing our route, we finally located the celebrated town whose center consisted of one small frame building which served as a combination store–post office. The man at the counter, however, said he lived eighty miles away and could not be of help. I felt it would be imprudent to wonder aloud if he was the postmaster. He said there was a phone booth near the building and I might try the local number.

To my surprise the phone was immediately answered. When I explained that I would like to come down, the man at the other end of the line said I was only half a mile away. He gave me careful directions and in a few minutes, after three turns, we proceeded down a dirt driveway into the woods toward what appeared to be a country residence. To be here looking for a map of Kilimanjaro seemed sufficiently absurd that I considered turning the car around for a get-a-way. But a thin man in a sweater was standing outside to greet us.

"So, you found your way," he called.

My inclination was to blurt out immediately how off the track we had gotten in searching for a map of Kilimanjaro. Perhaps he would be laughing hard enough to give me time to get away without prolonging the ordeal. But as I started on my confession, he stopped me short:

"We no longer have the contour map you're looking for. It's been out of print for many years. That was D.O.S. 522, done in the early sixties and published in sixty-five. It was on a 1:100,000 scale, about five-eighths of an inch to the mile. We had thousands of copies when Tanzania became independent, but one condition of the treaty was that no more copies would be printed and only those in stock would be distributed. We ran out of copies in the late seventies. Here, wait a minute, I'll show you what we're talking about."

Stunned, we watched him go into the house and return immediately to spread a copy of D.O.S. 522 on the "bonnet" of the car. This was the map I had seen at the Society, and I knew that standing before me was a worthy rival to Foyle's.

"We have only four copies left, and these things sell for £25 or £35."

"Could I buy it?"

"Absolutely not, they are our last and are definitely not for sale.

"These and other maps," he explained, "in fact, maps of the whole of Tanzania, were made by the D.O.S.—that's the British Director of Overseas Surveys—before independence. In fact, the D.O.S. has an even larger scale map, 1:50,000, or twice as detailed as this one. Here, I'll show you."

Back to the house he went, shortly reappearing with the larger scale map, which he also spread before us. Both maps had contour lines but, alas, neither showed the elevation of the Cave.

"The Cave's location was never pinpointed on these maps," he said, "and although the Tanzania government stated it was going to take care of its own mapping after independence, in fact, they have no money and have probably done nothing. There have been no maps made since the British left, or if there have been, they are militarily restricted and not available.

"You know, of course," he added, "that most countries have excellent maps which are done for military purposes.

But they are not available to the public. In your country, every square foot has been superbly mapped on a 1:25,000 scale; why, you can see the blokes walking in the street. The United States and many other countries are semi-military in their mapping expertise, but none of those maps can be gotten by the public. In any event, there is nothing more to be had anywhere on Kilimanjaro.

"By the way," he said, "which trail were you on? The Kibo trail goes to Gillman's Point but, you know, Uruhu Point is the real top. That's another walk around the crater."

He proceeded to describe the other trails, giving an astonishing cornucopia of particulars. I was sure he could have provided equal detail if we had asked about other parts of the earth, and listening to him I had the sure feeling there will always be an England.

When we recovered our equilibrium, I asked him about his company and its unaccountable location. He was Robin Collomb who, with his partner Anthony West, operated West-Col, a wholesale distributor of books and maps. Their warehouses were in Reading, and it had been my luck to catch him at home, where he happened to stop that day for lunch because of a business trip north that afternoon. He showed us a list of maps and books which his company distributes, pointing out the East African maps that had once been listed but were no longer available. It was not unusual, he said, for people searching for obscure maps to give up after scouring bookstores in their own countries and to telephone his company from all parts of the world, and at all hours of the day and night. The list he showed me included maps not only of Africa and the Himalayas, but of other parts of Asia, Europe, and, indeed, of everywhere on the globe. I knew, after listening to him, that I would not find any map with the detail I sought, unless it had been made by the Tanzania government itself, which I greatly doubted. As we drove away Collomb gave us a hearty wave, and I was satisfied we had exhausted the sources outside Africa itself.

Chapter 17
Questions Resolved

In the months after our return from Africa, I wondered why, when so many others had been on the mountain at the same time, no one else had suffered Effatta's fate, which had nearly been my own. I kept thinking, too, of the sick Japanese—who he was, and whether he had died alone.

The missionary, if he could be found, might have some answers. Remembering only that he was a Seventh Day Adventist from California, I called their office in New York and was referred to national headquarters in Washington. A charming woman promised to check, based on my sparse description. A week later she called to say that the man I was looking for was probably Keith Moses, and that he was returning to the United States in the summer of 1984. In midsummer, she reported that he was soon due in California and, later, gave me a temporary number. After many calls, I finally made contact.

He was indeed the man I sought, and was as affable and enthusiastic as he had been on Kilimanjaro. But he was not the novice climber I had assumed. Born in Wisconsin, he was raised in California and held a master's degree in industrial technology. He has been a Seventh Day Adventist teacher and missionary all his adult life. From 1971 to 1976 he was stationed in Peru; from 1976–79, he served in Ethiopia; and from 1979 until he returned to the United States in 1984, he was located in Kenya. He had three times climbed Mount Whitney, as well as other California peaks. In Peru, he had spent two weeks at an alpine training school and had then completed a sixteen-day expedition, with ice and rope climbing, to the 22,200-foot summit of Mount Huascarin. He had also climbed part way up Mount Kenya three times, as well as scaling Mount Elgon, in West Kenya. With this experience, and living at 6,800 feet in Kenya, he was well prepared, with a running and exercise program, for Kilimanjaro. He gave me a harrowing account of his climb.

When we started at 3:00 A.M., there were six of us—our guide and five of us hikers. We were the last group to leave the Kibo Hut, others having started as early as midnight. The night was clear and cold, about 0 degrees. We reached the Cave at 6:00 A.M. The slope was slippery and my guide, Emelee, a tall lanky fellow, said, "This is as far as we should go because it's too dangerous. I cannot be responsible for you from here on. If you want to go, you must go on alone."

Most of the people who had started from the hut had already turned back, many of them long before they reached the Cave. I decided to send my daughters back to the hut with some of the other hikers because the altitude was affecting them, and, besides, it was too dangerous.

I continued on up past the Cave alone. After about forty-five minutes, I heard a shout coming from above me, looked up, and saw a man sliding down the mountain. He shot past me, moaning and screaming. He went over some rocks that would send him bounding into the air and then he wouldn't hit the slope again for quite a number of feet. As he neared a rock pile he bounced over several more rocks that slowed him down, and by the time he went into the rock pile he was moving much slower. He hit it back first and his backpack took the shock so that he was not killed, as I had expected. He lay quite still.

Some of those in his party were trying to reach him without having the same thing happen to them. There was no trail, only the snow that had fallen a few days before and had partly melted into a slush which had then frozen solid,

212

making the side of the mountain extremely slippery and almost impossible to traverse. After fifteen or twenty minutes, the fallen man's friends got to him. I guess they were able to take him down to the Kibo Hut. I believe the man was a Belgian.

I continued on. About a half an hour after the Belgian fell, I heard another shout above me and looked up in time to see a rock the size of a baseball coming toward me. It swished by me and a moment later I heard it hit someone below. The man let out a groan. His companions were near him, and they caught him before he fell, but he must have had ribs or other bones broken. I kept a real vigil for fallen rocks from then on.

I continued on and finally reached the top about nine o'clock. The sun had come up shortly after 6:00 A.M., and I got some beautiful sunrise pictures as it rose behind Mawenzi.

I stayed at the top about an hour and a half. There was a cool breeze blowing, but the sun was hot and it started to melt some of the snow. It was still very slippery, but once I started down I was able to break through the crust and get my feet on the less-slippery portion beneath.*

Keith gave me the names of two Japanese. I assumed that they, like Keith, were a day ahead of us, and that they were unlikely to have any new information. Nevertheless, I wrote both, hoping to find the name of the Japanese who had died and to learn what schedule he had been on when he was taken ill, and how it came to be that he died alone.

Weeks went by with no word. Then one day a blue envelope arrived from Japan, the name of Shigeko Suzuki typed neatly in the upper left corner. As I read the letter, I

*Reprinted by permission of Keith Moses.

thought of Noguchi and Arashi, for Shigeko Suzuki's efforts were in the same tradition:

Dear Sir:
I'm sorry this letter is so late. And I'm afraid I cannot help you with so much information.

Anyway, I will tell you my experience in Kilimanjaro. Luckily, I know a Japanese. His name is Tsukada. He is a friend of that man who got sick at Kibo Hut and who was carried down. Tsukada took me a picture at Kibo-hut by chance. And after he came to Japan sent me the picture. So I had sent him a copy of your letter and I received his reply just a week ago.

Then I will write down my experience in Kilimanjaro in Japanese to avoid misunderstanding.

I hope you'll write a very nice book.

Regards,

Shigeko Suzuki*

Shigeko's account, which a friend of mine translated, added important detail. She was with a group of twenty-one, including six women. They had arrived in Tanzania on Tuesday, December 27, spent that night at the Kibo Hotel, and started climbing the next day. Wednesday night they were at the Mandara Huts, and they reached the Horombo Huts on Thursday afternoon. Perhaps due to their quick ascent, most in her party began to suffer from headaches. Friday morning, December 30, at about the same time as our party, they started for the Kibo Hut, arriving that same afternoon. All were then suffering from headaches and one

*Reprinted by permission of Shigeko (Suzuki) Nakata

woman, a Ms. Sano, was vomiting. She was given oxygen at the Kibo Hut.

Shigeko and her group left for the summit shortly before we did. She saw "the guide slip down and fall. . . . " She and her group then returned to the Kibo Hut; they were undoubtedly the Japanese with ice axes who had helped us descend. Soon thereafter they left for the Horombo Huts and came down to the Gate on New Year's Day. The woman who had been vomiting was carried down part way on the backs of various men, taking turns. Shigeko says that on New Year's Day "we by turns overcame and were overcome by a Japanese on a stretcher."

Shigeko had heard that a man named Jurata, one of her group, and another man, Tsukada, not of her group, had reached Gillman's Point. She thought they had climbed fast and gotten above the dangerous parts before the night cold had made the ice surface hard.

Tsukada's letter was longer and gave the full story of the sick Japanese. It is to Shigeko's effort that I owe the following account, which she copied for me:

My name is Fujio Tsukada. Our party consisted of three members, including myself, my friend Hisao Ishiguro, who was then twenty-seven, and a guide.

When we reached Horombo Hut, I had a bit of a headache and symptoms of altitude sickness had begun to show themselves. However, Ishiguro had no symptoms at all. The next morning we ate a hearty breakfast together and had no symptoms. At the last water point we both had a big drink of water. At this time I had a slight headache but Ishiguro was in fine shape. I checked his condition at that time so I am sure of it. An hour or so later, near a place called the Saddle, Ishiguro began to have a backache. We continued on and about thirty minutes before we reached the Kibo Hut, he took off his knapsack and rested. Soon thereafter he became unable to move. At this time, however, it was only a backache and he had no headache; we thought it was only the result of drinking water too fast. Our guide came back and carried his knapsack for him.

After we arrived at the Kibo Hut, and while he was trying to sleep, he was unable to breathe and so, it still being daylight, we lay him outside where he could be hit by the rays of the sun. At this time too he was suffering only from backaches. At dusk we thought we would have something to eat and then sleep, but Ishiguro began to vomit. On the advice of the guide we gave him only hot water. At about 5:30 P.M. he again tried to sleep. He did not vomit and was breathing normally while he slept.

At about midnight I woke him up so that we could be off, but he was extremely drowsy. The guide recommended letting him rest, so the guide and I set off for the summit. We reached the summit early in the morning and then returned to the Kibo Hut, arriving there about 7:50 A.M. We discovered that Ishiguro's condition had worsened and he was fading in and out of consciousness. Upon consultation with the guide, we went to the hut attendants and obtained a stretcher to carry him down. The guide went ahead and accompanied him next to the stretcher.

I went separately and, to preserve my strength, decided to spend the night at the Horombo Hut and to descend to the Gate the next day. When I reached the Horombo Hut, Ishiguro was there. He is a man of considerable physical strength and on the way to the Horombo Hut he had regained consciousness. It was possible for him to stand on his feet but he was not able to do so. However his speech and memory were normal. We tested in various ways, having him for instance try to touch his left leg with his right hand, which he did. I thought that he was recovering. He ate dinner and slept, but in the middle of the night his condition worsened again. He would toss off his sleeping bag and blanket and he appeared as if he were racked in agony. I replaced the sleeping bag and blankets but he had the seizures four or five times during the night.

In the morning he was slipping in and out of conscious-ness and I knew it was necessary to get him down by stretcher. The guide again accompanied Ishiguro down the mountain, and I was instructed to go ahead by myself to the Gate.

I later learned that as he was brought down to the Gate, he was accompanying the body of the dead guide and that he, Ishiguro, was taken in the same truck that went partway to the Mandara Hut to pick up the dead guide.

At the Gate I met Ishiguro and he weakly responded to my calling his name. A member of the rescue group said his consciousness would return soon. But since he did not revive, we decided to take him directly to the hospital. He was in the Kilimanjaro Christian Medical Center from Janu-ary 1 to January 7. On January 4 he regained consciousness and on January the 7th he was discharged. He did not die. We were given a lift in the car of an American connected with the International School going to Arusha. There we got a bus carrying a group of Japanese tourists to Nairobi. We left Nairobi on January 8, spent one night in Pakistan, and returned home to Japan.

Now the night I was ascending to the summit, while Ishiguro remained at the Kibo Hut, there was a Japanese physician also climbing to the summit. He had spent the night at the Kibo Hotel on December 27 as we did, and, like us, he expected to reach the summit early on the morning of December 31. At a point just below where the guide died, the Japanese physician was stricken with altitude sickness and was carried down. I believe he was carried to the Gate on December 31. This was probably the man that Mr. Hartzell saw being taken down in the dark. I met this man in Moshi on January 2 or 3 and so he did not die either.*

*Reprinted by permission of Fujio Tsukada.

Shigeko Suzuki and Fujio Tsukada at the Kibo Hut. Roland at far right

I read Tsukada's account with joy, and with a prayer of thanks that Ishiguro had survived. Someday I would like to shake his hand and tell him how glad I am that he is alive and healthy. He was not, after all, the man I saw being taken down in the dark. It remains unclear how reports of the death of a Japanese climber could have circulated in Tanzania; perhaps there was still another climber who died. But at least I now knew that the man whose fate had so troubled me did, in fact, survive, and there was relief in knowing that the African guides did not commit the terrible error of losing a life by failing to move him down the mountain soon enough. Still, Ishiguro's experience drives home the lesson that altitude sickness demands immediate and unhesitating descent—not the sporadic descent that kept him one night at the Kibo Hut, and another night at Horombo. Once pulmonary edema begins, descent is imperative; one's condition deteriorates with increasing speed every moment of delay. He was close to death because of delay. No climber should forget the lesson.

The happy news from Japan cleared up the last major question of the drama. By a fortunate coincidence I received, a few days later, a note from Miss C. J. B. Mmari of the Kilimanjaro National Park stating: "I would like to inform you that the Hans Meyer Cave is at an altitude of 17,045 ft. above sea level." So, I had come to the end of the adventure which, by any measure, had been extraordinary, and which few like us will ever experience. It will be retold, time and again, by those who were there, and it needs no embellishment. And I delight in the thought that when our grandchildren observe us, sitting placid and content at some future Christmas dinner, they will have this account to remind them that our family holidays were not always uneventful.

There may even be more. Tom called the other day and asked, "Where *exactly* is Mount Ararat?"

Bibliography

Bauer, Yehuda. *A History of the Holocaust.* New York: Franklin Watts, 1982.

Brown, Leslie. *Africa, A Natural History.* New York: Random House, 1985.

Davidson, Basil. *The Growth of African Civilization, East and Central Africa to the Late Nineteenth Century.* London: Longman Group Ltd., 1967.

Fisher, Arthur. *The Healthy Heart.* Alexandria, Virginia: Time-Life Books, 1981.

Frank, Anne. *The Diary of a Young Girl.* New York: Pocketbooks, a division of Simon and Schuster Inc., 1958.

Frank, Anne. *The Diary of a Young Girl.* New York: Pocketbooks, Simon and Schuster Division of Gulf & Western Corporation, 1972.

Gunther, John. *Inside Africa.* New York: Harper and Brothers, 1953.

Houston, Charles S., M.D. *Going High—The Story of Man and Altitude.* New York: The American Alpine Club, 1980.

Mountaineering, the Freedom of the Hills. (Fourth Edition.) Seattle, Washington: The Mountaineers, 1982.

Safari, Dr. J. F. *Swahili Made Easy.* Dar es Salaam: Tanzania Publishing House, 1980.

Saibull, Solomon ole and Rachel Carr. *A Herd & Spear.* London: Collins and Harwill Press, 1981.

Schnabel, Ernst. *Anne Frank, a Portrait in Courage.* New York: Harcourt, Brace and Company, 1968.

Selye, Hans, M.D. *The Stress of Life.* New York: McGraw Hill, 1978.

Parish, Thomas, ed. *Encyclopedia of World War II.* New York: Simon and Schuster, 1978.

Willcock, Colin and the editors of Time-Life Books. *The World's Wild Places; Africa's Rift Valley.* Netherlands: Time-Life International, 1974.